KINGDOM
CALLING

KINGDOM CALLING

The Vocation, Ministry and Discipleship
of the Whole People of God

The Faith and Order Commission

Church House Publishing
Church House
Great Smith Street
London SW1P 3AZ
www.chpublishing.co.uk

Published 2020 for the Faith and Order Commission
of the Church of England by Church House Publishing

Copyright © The Archbishops' Council 2020

ISBN 978 0 7151 1176 5 (Paperback)

ISBN 978 0 7151 1177 2 (Core Source eBook)

ISBN 978 0 7151 1178 9 (Kindle Edition)

GS Misc 1254

British Library Cataloguing in Publication Data

A catalogue record for this book is available from
the British Library

Typeset by ForDesign

Printed and bound by CPI Group (UK) Ltd, Croydon, CR0 4YY

Contents

Preface

by Christopher Cocksworth
Bishop of Coventry
Chair, Faith and Order Commission

The Faith and Order Commission welcomed the call to work with others to 'Enrich the theology' that was made when *Setting God's People Free* was presented to the General Synod in 2017. Partnership with the Setting God's People Free team and with Ministry Council and the staff who support it has already borne fruit in the publication last year of *Calling All God's People*. *Kingdom Calling* is a rather different kind of text, aiming to 'Enrich the theology' by addressing half-hidden habits of thought that inhibit the realization of our theological ideals about the vocation, ministry, and discipleship of all God's people.

A number of the Commission's members have been especially closely involved in preparing *Kingdom Calling*, including Anne Hollinghurst, who chaired the Steering Group for the project, and Loveday Alexander and Joshua Hordern who were members of it, while Jeremy Worthen served as secretary. It has been, however, very much a collaborative endeavour, and many people have contributed their insights, including members of the Ministry Council and its Lay Ministries Advisory Group and members of the Setting God's People Free Advisory Group. The presentations and the responses to them from participants at the Lambeth Palace colloquium on *Calling All God's People in July* 2019 provided a crucial catalyst for this second text, while Nicholas Townsend lent invaluable editorial scrutiny when it was nearing completion.

The Commission has been very conscious that many important books have been written on these subjects, and indeed continue to be produced. This is not an attempt to compete in either inspirational content or weight of scholarship, but to help the Church of England do the sort of theological work necessary to undergird the prayer for all God's people:

Almighty and everlasting God,
by whose Spirit the whole body of the Church
   is governed and sanctified:
hear our prayer which we offer for all your faithful people,
that in their vocation and ministry
they may serve you in holiness and truth
to the glory of your name;
through our Lord and Saviour Jesus Christ.

Collect for the ministry of all Christian people, Common Worship

Foreword

by Eve Poole

Third Church Estates Commissioner

Kingdom Calling asks a very difficult question: what is the point of all of these worthy Church of England reports, if they have no effect? This one looks at why, despite all the good work done over so many years to rehabilitate the role of the laity, so little has changed. It's our chance to break this cycle and prove we can plot an alternative future, and to use this report as a spur to deliberate and sustained action to recognize the legitimacy of the ministry of all the baptized.

Perhaps this is the *kairos* moment for *Kingdom Calling*. The Church is poised to embrace a new Quinquennial Vision and Strategy based on the Five Marks of Mission.

> **To proclaim the Good News of the Kingdom**
>
> **To teach, baptise and nurture new believers**
>
> **To respond to human need by loving service**
>
> **To seek to transform unjust structures of society, to challenge violence of every kind and to pursue peace and reconciliation**
>
> **To strive to safeguard the integrity of creation and sustain and renew the life of the earth**

The Five Marks are often abbreviated to Tell, Teach, Tend, Transform and Treasure. The current Renewal and Reform agenda has perhaps necessarily emphasised the first two, being based on research that shows that the best way to increase the number of disciples is to raise up more priests, which emphasises the clericalism this FAOC report is at pains to counter. But a re-framing of the Church of England's activity using the Five Marks naturally includes the entire family of the baptized.

While it may be that those called to ordination are best placed to lead us in the Telling and Teaching, we can all Tend, Transform and Treasure, and indeed the laity are often better placed to be active in these latter spheres. The Archbishop of York talks about a 'mixed ecology' church, which includes the whole range of ministries, ordained and lay, parish-based or through chaplaincy, and throughout all the situations and places of England.

As the Church by law established, we have responsibility for the cure of all the souls of England, which is why Archbishop William Temple reminded us that we exist for those who are not our members, as well as for those who are. It feels that the time is now ripe to heed the call of this report to more manifestly embrace our vocation and discipleship in all of these areas – particularly in a post-Covid world and in recognition of the institutional racism that besets our structures – so that we may begin afresh to answer the call of the Kingdom.

Introduction

Origins

In February 2017, the Church of England's General Synod approved the recommendations of *Setting God's People Free*, a report from the Archbishops' Council that had been produced by the Lay Leadership Task Group. The report highlighted concerns around the continuing marginalization of lay leadership and discipleship in the life of the Church of England. It identified a need to take action to establish

> A culture that communicates the all-encompassing scope of the good news for the whole of life, and pursues the core calling of every church community – and every follower of Jesus – to form whole-life maturing disciples. And a culture that embodies in every structure and way of working the mutuality of our baptismal calling and fruitful complementarity of our roles and vocations.[1]

This report made it clear that theological work had a critical role in enabling the culture change it called for. Its chapter on 'Constraining Factors' began by identifying 'A Theological Deficit', explaining that

> Without proper theological undergirding, it will be impossible to form and nurture Christians who are capable of proclaiming and living out the gospel in their daily lives, engaging confidently and faithfully with the complex challenges of today, and becoming an effective presence for Christ in their communities.[2]

Correspondingly, the first of the 'Levers for Change' listed in the following chapter was 'Theologically grounded identity and vision for lay people', while the second priority in the 'High Level Implementation Plan' provided in the first Annex was 'Enrich the theology'. Faith and Order Commission staff were mentioned as one of the 'owners' of this priority and associated actions. Meanwhile, a separate initiative led by the Lay Ministries Working Group had concluded that there was a need for culture change within the Church of England in this area too, proposing that it would require a commitment to deepen 'corporate and institutional reflection' on the role of lay ministry in the Church of England and on the most fruitful forms of support for the flourishing of this ministry at parish, diocesan and national levels.[3]

Since 2017, the Church of England's Faith and Order Commission has been working in partnership with the Setting God's People Free team and with the Ministry Council and its staff to address the theological deficit that had been identified in both contexts. That work led to the writing of a theological overview document designed to present in concise and accessible form some 'theological undergirding' that could serve both areas of work. The text, published as *Calling All God's People* in July 2019 as part of the Setting God's People Free suite of resources, reflected the collaborative nature of its production in the juxtaposition of the Commission's words with stories, reflections and questions prepared by the Setting God's People Free team. It drew together theological insights that the Commission believes to be vital for renewing all God's people in their calling.[4]

Also published in 2019 was a document from the Church of England's Ministry Council, called 'Ministry for a Christian Presence in Every Community'.[5] It was written to contribute to an extensive discussion in the Church of England on how to understand and enable the whole people of God to be active and engaged in God's mission in God's world. There was therefore a profound congruence between this text and *Calling All God's People*. With different but complementary emphases, 'Ministry for a Christian Presence in Every Community' presents a powerful theological exhortation for the whole people of God to share together in the mission of God in the world:

> We are called to participate in and be transfigured by the dynamic being of the Triune God. Through God's work of creation, Jesus' incarnation and the gift of the Spirit we know God as relating and sending to realise God's Kingdom. This relating and sending is God's mission into which the Church is called to be wholeheartedly, as witness and agent. Ministers serve God's mission by enabling the Church's participation, through the energising power of the Spirit.[6]

Throughout this partnership, however, between the Faith and Order Commission, the Setting God's People Free team and the Ministry Council, there has been a nagging sense that presenting good theology – the aim of the overview text – is not quite enough. As *Setting God's People Free* had observed, there has been a notable sequence of Church of England reports since the mid-twentieth century on affirming, supporting and growing the participation of the laity in the mission and ministry of the church, with much good theology

2

outlined within them; and yet the concerns in this area keep recurring.[7] While of course there are practical issues that need to be addressed here, e.g. around policy priorities and the allocation of resources, that is not the whole story. The good theology presented in these reports has failed to capture people's imagination across the church in a way that changes the way they think of themselves in relation to others and give value to different activities, and that failure is bound up with the lack of impact on behaviour and decision-making. To address the question of why this has been so requires a theological response. Providing that is the central purpose of the present report.

Nonetheless, in the specific case of lay ministries that are licensed, authorized, or commissioned, there has been remarkable growth in recent years in terms of both the numbers of people involved and the proliferation of different categories. Research currently being conducted for the Church of England's Lay Ministry Data Project has gathered over 1,300 different role titles from an initial survey of dioceses, which have then been categorized into 40 distinct groupings.[8] The range of people responding to God's call by offering themselves for ministries of many different kinds is something to be celebrated, as is the evidence of human creativity and the energy of the Holy Spirit in opening up new avenues of service. Nonetheless, this development also raises theological questions, not least about consistency in the way ministry is understood and the relationship between lay and ordained forms of it. Moreover, there has been a recurring concern that the welcome given to lay ministries is not always followed through consistently, with attitudes persisting in which ordained ministry is ultimately at the centre, and everything else secondary and supportive at best, peripheral and distracting at worst.

There is, therefore, a case for a different kind of theological work to complement that which has already been done: work that, to use medical metaphors, can be described as 'diagnostic' and 'healing'. The two are inseparable from one another: only by understanding what is wrong can we find the right path forward. Why has it proved so difficult for changes that all apparently agree to be necessary and important actually to take root in the life of the Church of England – or in the terms of *Setting God's People Free*, why has the culture proved so difficult to shift when there is no obvious argument being put forward in favour of the status quo? Accepting our need for healing in how we imagine and understand ourselves as God's representatives in God's world and as the one body of Christ's church is pivotal for addressing this. With confidence in the one who came not for the healthy but for the sick, we need to seek Jesus' understanding of our malady and then walk with him into the healing he alone can bring, in the renewal of our minds and in the wholeness of our life together as God's people.

The major goal of this report, then, is to articulate a theological diagnosis of this enduring resistance to embracing the discipleship and ministry of the whole church, and to identify pathways to healing that may help to overcome it. The patterns of theological thinking involved in this diagnosis and healing do not exist on a separate plane from everyday reality but are in continual interaction with social movements and cultural change, as well as moral action and indeed moral failure on the part of both institutions and individuals. The interchange between theology, society and culture is a recurring theme in the three main chapters of the report, which focus in turn on the vocation, *ministry and discipleship* of all God's people, asking what may be inhibiting them and what kind of theological thinking and imagining might most help them to flourish. Before turning to that task, however, the next two sections of the Introduction consider in more detail the symptoms that make such a diagnosis necessary, offering an outline of key elements arising from it that will inform the approach of the chapters that follow.

Outlining the symptoms

The idea that the renewal of the church for mission in the context of modernity hinges on enabling the fuller participation of the laity became widespread in the decades following the Second World War, although its roots could be traced back further. It was an integral part of a number of movements that reached the peak of their influence during that time. It formed one of the guiding principles of the Liturgical Movement, for instance. During the same period, the Ecumenical Movement grew increasingly prominent as a movement of renewal for mission that gave considerable scope for lay leadership and involvement, while also providing a forum for the exchange of ideas on lay participation; seminal publications on this subject from the 1950s were widely read across the denominations.[9] The Second Vatican Council produced documents that drew positively on both of these movements as agents for ecclesial renewal, affirming the central role of the laity in the church's mission in the world.[10] Its texts were eagerly read by many non-Roman Catholic Christians around the world as convergent with their deepest hopes and prayers.[11]

While the Council was meeting in the 1960s, two widely influential books by academic theologians on the role of the laity were published. Kathleen Bliss's *We the People* situated its vision of the laity in the post-war global ecumenical movement.[12] At the same time, it also emphasized that articulate, confident lay people were vital for the church's mission in a rapidly secularizing social context. Bliss argued that there was too much focus on lay people carrying out supportive work within worshipping communities at the expense of their role in wider society. She queried whether church leadership was equipping lay people sufficiently to understand their faith and to explain it to others, arguing that – thus equipped – laity could help to bridge the widening gap between the church and a secularizing culture. Similar points were made in Gibb and Morton's seminal volume, *God's Frozen People*.[13] Published in the same year, it argued that the laity were best equipped to reinvigorate evangelism in Western society, at a point where the clergy appeared to have largely lost the necessary skills and understanding.

A similar perspective had informed a major report from the Church of England written almost two decades earlier. *Towards the Conversion of England*, published just after the Second World War, focused on the need for lay people to be motivated and ready for the challenges of evangelization in a secularizing society.[14] A major theme was 'The Apostolate of the Whole Church', and the report also made it clear that there needed to be appropriate training and support for lay people as they engaged in evangelism and witness day by day. There is clear continuity between this work and the *Lambeth Essays on Ministry* published as one of three volumes of preparatory studies for the bishops attending the 1968 Lambeth Conference, alongside collections of essays on 'Faith' and on 'Unity'. The writers built on statements made at the 1958 Lambeth Conference that affirmed the primary calling of the laity as 'serving [God] in their daily work and witness'. While allowing that this might involve callings to serve in the 'mission fields' overseas, the essays sought to emphasize the need to recognize secularizing Western societies such as England as locations of essentially the same kind, with clergy needing to be focused on supporting the laity in their challenging task of witness within this context.[15]

One initiative that emerged in the early 1960s in the Church of England that was evidently driven by this current of thinking was the founding of the Southwark Ordination Course. Inspired by the Worker Priest movement in post-war Roman Catholicism in Continental Europe, it sought to enable men to remain grounded in the culture of their work place and associated community while preparing for and then exercising ordained ministry, so that they would be able to minister in new ways to those who would be 'serving [God] in their daily work and witness' from within that same culture and community.[16] There was a specific awareness of the need to address the distance that was perceived to have grown between the prevailing clerical culture, sustained by the traditional theological colleges, and the culture of working-class estates in south London.

Within ten years, a national network had emerged of similar institutions and a formal recognition of 'non-stipendiary ministry' within the Church of England. Yet the focus had also shifted too, away from forming ministers who would share in the social circumstances, including the daily work, of those they were serving, to finding a new source of voluntary help in maintaining existing patterns of public worship and associated activities. The vision of a new pattern of ordained ministry whose priority would be supporting lay witness and discipleship from a place of social solidarity had been largely lost.[17] One of the motivations for the subsequent introduction of 'Ordained Local Ministry' was to recapture that vision, but it has continued to prove difficult to sustain. The continuing question that first comes into sharp focus in the nineteenth-century of the relationship between ordained ministry and the general social category of 'professionals', with its associated expectations about training, forms part of the background here.[18]

Two decades later, it was evident to some that the enthusiastic consensus of the 1960s had failed to change the underlying situation in the Church of England regarding the participation of the laity in ministry and mission. *All Are Called*, published in 1985, argued that lay people were still seen primarily as 'non-ordained' and their roles and ministries subordinate to those of the clergy.[19] It criticized the church for being preoccupied with its own ecclesiastical structures rather than attending to its fundamental task of transforming the world. Having set out a categorization of different kinds of lay ministry, including 'churchly ministries', 'ministries with family, friends and neighbours', 'Monday morning ministries' and 'Saturday night' ministries, it called for the

Church of England to acknowledge and value their worth alongside the ministries of the ordained, and not as inferior to them.

All Are Called served as a catalyst for renewed attention on the role of the laity, and in particular on the need for adult Christian education. Ten years after its publication, however, one of its contributors commented:

> for a time there was a flurry of activity, and some major work – notably in liturgy... but over recent years the Anglican focus on such issues as the ordination of women distracted energy from the task, and surveying the scene one is tempted to mourn how little headway has been made.[20]

When another Working Group from the Board of Education, which had been responsible for *All Are Called*, issued a progress document in 1999 on relevant initiatives, it had to acknowledge that after a flurry of activity in the late 1980s, funding for lay development posts had been cut and the Church of England's strategic focus had moved towards ordained and Reader ministries. Despite the progress which they agreed had been made, the report's writers noted that 'There is a deep and profoundly disturbing gap between intention, strategy and the reality of what is actually happening in many parishes.'[21]

One might see the same pattern replicated in the reception of what became known as the Hind Report, its original title being *Formation for Ministry in a Learning Church*.[22] Published in 2003, one of its key recommendations was for widely available courses under the umbrella of 'Education for Discipleship', designed to enable people who were seeking to grow in discipleship and ministry to benefit from learning in the context of the Church of England's network of Theological Education Institutions, without requiring any intention of serving as ordained or licensed lay ministers. Such courses were also to be made mandatory for those in the process of discerning a calling to these ministries, thus affirming the common ground of all particular vocations in the shared call of discipleship. The proposal would have required either additional resources or the moving of funding from other budgets to implement it. With rising costs for initial training for ordination, a determination on many sides to protect expenditure in this area and a desire to move suitable candidates into ordained ministry as quickly as possible given the declining numbers of stipendiary ministers, the recommendation of 'Education for Discipleship' looked like an unrealistic aspiration. It quietly disappeared from view.

The seeds of *Setting God's People Free*, which provided the catalyst for work leading to the current report, were sown in 2011 in a debate at the General Synod, on a report from the Archbishops' Council and the House of Bishops called 'Challenges for the New Quinquennium'.[23] The report again drew attention to the 'importance of lay development', not in connection with ecclesial roles or church planting but for 'equipping members of the laity for effective discipleship in the world'. Concerns in this area continued to be raised within the House of Laity in particular over the next few years. From 2015 onwards, they were channelled into the Renewal and Reform initiative (originally called Reform and Renewal) launched by the Archbishops of Canterbury and York at the February sessions of the General Synod that year and focused on promoting the growth of the church in mission. In that context, it is not surprising that the sense of urgency about mobilizing the laity for evangelization that had marked *Towards the Conversion of England* in 1945 now returned to the forefront, as is evident from the opening paragraphs of *Setting God's People Free* itself:

> A great opportunity lies before us. It is the same opportunity that has presented itself to the Church in every decade for the last 100 years. It is an opportunity that arguably has not been fully grasped since the days of Wesley.

> Will we determine to empower, liberate and disciple the 98% of the Church of England who are not ordained and therefore set them free for fruitful, faithful mission and ministry, influence, leadership and, most importantly, vibrant relationship with Jesus in all of life? And will we do so not only in church-based ministry on a Sunday but in work and school, in gym and shop, in field and factory, Monday to Saturday?[24]

As already noted, the authors of *Setting God's People Free* were aware of the cyclical nature of the Church of England's engagement in this area since the 1940s: well-received reports stimulate new ideas and initiatives, which within a couple of decades – or rather less – have lost momentum as their limited impact becomes apparent. To avoid the same fate, the report rightly focused on the need to have a clear plan for implementation, based on identifying and addressing 'Constraining Factors', the title of its third chapter. What the Faith and Order Commission offers in the current text is a deepening of that analysis, outlining the theological and spiritual work that is needed to overcome the forces of inertia that have proved so powerful over the past seventy years.

Towards a diagnosis

Dynamics of secularization

Why is it that concerns about valuing and nurturing the participation of all God's people in mission and ministry have proved so remarkably persistent in the Church of England, in spite of the widespread consensus about the urgency of addressing them and the many positive initiatives of the last fifty years? At least part of the answer lies in the way they are intertwined with the dynamics of 'secularization', itself a deeply contested term.[25] Casanova's influential analysis distinguished three strands in studies of secularization: the differentiation of social space into autonomous spheres, with religious institutions losing the power to determine understanding and behaviour beyond their limited domain; the privatization of religion, with religious voices ceasing to have influence in politics and the public square more generally; and the decline of religious belief, practice and affiliation, with associated reductions in scale of religious communities and institutions. Reflecting on the radically altered profile of religion in global politics during the 1980s, Casanova contended that while it had been argued that modernization of societies made all three forms of secularization inevitable, in fact only the first – differentiation – was integral to modernization.[26]

Church leaders in this country, as elsewhere in Western Europe since the Second World War, have been sharply conscious of secularization, without necessarily disentangling the different threads in how it is presented in social science. Casanova's analysis is useful in illuminating how the phenomenon of secularization has drawn contrasting responses from the churches in the post-war decades. Secularization as differentiation marks the eclipse of Christendom, conceived as a society in which a Christian church is favoured by the state, whose authorities are members of that church and give it comprehensive formal and informal influence in political and cultural life. Few would argue that this shift is a straightforwardly negative development.

9

It clarifies the character of the 'saeculum' – the duration of human history – as the time in which different loves and loyalties are in a contest for the hearts of people. The clearing away of the appearance of a devoted Christian nation and the emerging of thought-forms running counter to Christian faith make it harder to be Christian, and especially unreflectively Christian. Yet they also open a space of freedom within which reflective, intentional discipleship can be fostered, and the church can find its place in an open public square alongside other voices and other actors. On the other hand, secularization as privatization of religion and secularization as decline in religion present more obviously direct challenges to the churches. These may be felt most sharply in the case of those such as the Church of England that had held a privileged place in public life and secure access to material resources in the Christendom era.

Two related effects of the dynamics of secularization provide crucial context for the series of publications and initiatives reviewed in the previous section: the perceived weakening of Christian influence in political, social, and cultural life, and the progressive diminishment in church membership and material resources. In both cases, it is not difficult to understand why fostering the full participation of the laity would be considered vital for any serious attempt to combat or at least mitigate these effects. In a society where ecclesiastical office and theological knowledge no longer carry authority beyond their limited social spheres, those whose place in other areas of public life rests on their routine involvement and specialist expertise within them must take responsibility for exercising Christian influence and maintaining a Christian presence there. Hence the need to support lay discipleship. In a church where clergy are struggling to maintain the worshipping communities and associated institutions that they have inherited, lay people are increasingly crucial both for drawing in new members and for making the demands of ministry bearable by taking on new roles and responsibilities within their worshipping communities. Hence the need to support lay ministry.

Clear lines can be drawn, then, between some of the more obvious perceived effects of secularization and the concern to promote lay discipleship and lay ministry since the Second World War. Those lines also suggest where we might look for signs of what has made that support less effective than has been repeatedly hoped. If support for lay discipleship and ministry is motivated by concern to address certain losses for the church associated with secularization, then if those losses could be either reversed or addressed in some other way, would such support then cease? Supposing, for instance, the case was made that more effective clerical leadership was in fact the key to regaining Christian influence in public life and to growing worshipping communities: would the call to promote fuller lay involvement in discipleship and ministry remain so compelling? While the impact of secularization may bestow an urgency on enabling the participation of the whole people of God in the whole work of God, it cannot create a fundamental imperative. Unless that imperative is understood and grasped as one that arises from the heart of Christian faith, then support for change to enable greater participation by the laity will always be vulnerable to erosion when someone claims to have a superior tactic for addressing the church's problems. It will also be clouded by the feeling that it is an unfortunate necessity that adverse circumstances have forced upon us, rather than a joyful response to the abundance of God's gift. Has the Church of England as a whole really understood and embraced the theological imperative for the participation of the whole people of God in the whole work of God?

The complexity of secularization as analysed by Casanova and others also, however, indicates why advocacy of lay discipleship and ministry has faced some powerful headwinds over that same period. Most obviously, secularization as differentiation and secularization as privatization inevitably affect the thinking of religious people in far-reaching ways, and not only those identifying as having no religion. They mean that Christians imbibe, without being especially conscious of it, a mentality that shrinks faith's authority and relevance to the limited domain of its recognized social institutions on the one hand and privatized individual religious practice on the other. Once that mentality takes hold, exhortations to church members to live the life of discipleship day by day in every part of life will struggle to find purchase in minds and hearts. This is not a matter of such appeals being consciously dismissed or resisted, but rather of them appearing to be operating on a plane that does not readily connect with the world as it is actually seen to be. Moreover, within that limited domain of public religious institutions and private religious practice, it seems evident that those with the professional skills and the acknowledged authority to maintain the institutions and advise on the practice are very much at the centre of things. That is likely to mean, first and foremost, the clergy, however much they might benefit in these tasks from the assistance of lay people in secondary and supporting roles. The effects of secularization, then, in the loss of Christian influence and church membership point to the vital importance of lay discipleship and lay ministry. Yet at the same time, the effects of secularization on the way we all see the world undermine the plausibility both of the relevance of discipleship to the whole of life and of the equality in mutuality of all ministries.

Three critical factors

Three critical factors can be identified as showing how secularization as thus understood affects our theological thinking in ways that are directly relevant for the participation of the whole people of God in the whole work of God. Together, these three factors provide the outline of the diagnosis that is explored in the chapters that follow. The first is a weakness of theological imagination regarding the relationship between the cardinal Christian doctrines of creation and salvation and the realities of daily life in human society. When we labour under an anaemic vision of God's world and Christ's saving work, we struggle to see ourselves in our regular occupations, duties and pleasures as living out our divinely given callings as those created in the divine image and redeemed by the blood of Christ, who is now risen and reigning, and in whom all things now hold together (Col. 1.17). We are inclined to see that calling instead more properly expressed in 'spiritual' activities and 'ministerial' work. And so we conform in our minds to the pattern of this world (Rom. 12.2), in which the good news of Christ is tolerated so long as it is restricted to private places of voluntary association or the believer's inner world, but is excluded from relevance to the world which God has made and on which he has set his love, sealed forever in the blood of Christ. In short, we acquiesce as the public significance of the gospel is suppressed and our witness to Christ is thus diminished. In what follows, this factor is a particular focus in the first chapter, on vocation.

The second factor is an impoverishment of our understanding of the church. The ease with which 'church' is sometimes contrasted with, for example, mission, world or kingdom betrays a lack of appreciation for the fullness of the mystery of the church in Christian teaching, and its inseparability from the mission of the Triune God, the purposes of God for the world and the coming of the kingdom of God. On the other hand, too sharp a distinction between the 'gathered' and the 'sent' church can raise a certain tension as to how these two 'modes' of church relate to one another, which may then be resolved, somewhat unsatisfactorily, by asserting the relative priority of one mode to the other. The church exists as a network of social institutions at local, regional, national, and international levels – but the category of institution cannot exhaust its reality as sign, instrument and foretaste of God's reign, and thinking about both 'church and world' and 'clergy and laity' needs to be undertaken with the fullness of that reality as its horizon. Moreover, perceptions that clergy are defined by their identification with the church as institution, or that the church as institution somehow sits above or aside from all other institutions within a society, clearly need to be challenged. Indeed, theological depictions of 'church and world' that imply a simplistic separation between two realms tend to generate a division between 'clergy and laity' that we will inevitably then struggle to overcome. Not surprisingly, therefore, this factor is the subject of careful attention in the second chapter, on ministry.

The third factor, closely related to the first two, is disorientation in judging how to respond to the ever-shifting currents of our culture – discerning where they need to be resisted and where they ought to be celebrated. To accept secularization as differentiation is to recognize that the church does not hold authority over the social order, and that the pervasively influential ideas in our culture will not be expressed in the language of faith and may be at cross-purposes with the church's self-understanding and mission. And yet they cannot be simply dismissed for that reason. The church maintains that the whole of human life, especially its social expressions, belongs within God's creation, and that the church is called to be truly and transformatively present in every human culture. This means that Christians cannot either uncritically acquiesce to or reject prevailing attitudes and assumptions, or indeed be willing to live by different truths in the 'religious' compartment of their lives from other dimensions of them. Instead, we must discern what God's good, acceptable and perfect will is for our lives (Rom. 12.2). The challenges for such discernment are significant. For the perplexity which our disorientation and compartmentalization generate extends to how we frame our thinking about discipleship and ministry, where attitudes and assumptions circulating within society about work, worth and fulfilment are likely to influence us, whether consciously or not. How may the complex representations of reality which are influential in any given time and societal context be preventing us from hearing, celebrating, and supporting God's call to all God's people? What are we to make, for instance, of tendencies in our society to fill its members' time with the demands of economic work, subtle pressures to compete and self-promote across every sphere of life and endless offers of cultural products for our time-consuming consumption? How do we respond to habits of assessing people's worth based on the use they are to others, rendering those apparently useless – the very young, the seriously sick and the very old – thereby worthless? We are bound to be influenced by these developments to some extent, whether we recognize it and resist it, recognize it and accept it or simply do not notice it much at all. Do they reflect anything positive, or is it our duty simply to oppose them – and how would we do that? Although this factor is relevant to all three of the chapters that follow, it comes into the foreground in the final chapter especially, on discipleship.

Taken together, these three factors, to do with daily life and work, the church, and cultural context, make a powerful combination: a weakness of theological imagination in how Christians see their involvement in society, a limited understanding of the mystery of the church, and disorientation in the face of powerful currents within our culture about worth, work and fulfilment. In different ways, they all reflect the influence of the mentality associated with secularization that limits the authority and relevance of faith to its recognized social institutions and privatized individual practice. This mentality has the potential to affect profoundly how those who profess faith in Christ as Lord of all see themselves, the church and the world, in ways that may pass unnoticed and indeed interact with aspects of their theological thinking, yet still stand in tension with their profession. Exploring that process is critical for understanding the disease for which we are seeking pathways of healing. As we lose confidence in everyday life as the place where the adventure of discipleship unfolds, so our picture of the church correspondingly shrinks and it becomes difficult to keep its various dimensions in proportion, including the relationship between different forms of ministry.

This initial diagnosis is developed in more detail in the following chapters, which also point the way towards the corresponding pathways to healing. Such healing will draw on the treasures of Christian doctrine. Weakness of theological imagination about daily life and work emphasizes the importance of the doctrine of creation for understanding human beings as social and cultural creatures. A limited conception of the church highlights the need for a consistently missional ecclesiology to help us expand our vision. In seeking orientation so that we can respond as faithful disciples to cultural trends and their deeper dynamics in a secularizing society, our Christology should give us confidence in the presence and work of the risen Christ, who promises to accompany and guide us in every part of life.

Clearly, these factors do not solely affect the Church of England; to some degree all Christian communities in this country need to address them. It may be, however, that there are particular features of the Church of England's history, inherited institutions and current situation that leave it more exposed than other churches to one or more of these factors, as there may be other features that give it important resources to draw on in addressing them. Learning from and with the whole Church of God – not just in this country but worldwide – has to be an integral part of the healing that we are looking for.

Overview

The theological overview document from the Faith and Order Commission referred to earlier, *Calling All God's People*, sought to sketch out concisely how the rhythm of the church in commissioning for service and dwelling in communion embraces three critical themes: calling, discipleship and ministry. The present more extended report, designed primarily for those with responsibilities for preaching, teaching and training in the Church of England, also has three main chapters linked to the same three themes, while acknowledging that they cannot be neatly separated. It develops some of the core ideas presented in that overview text, by expounding them in greater depth and by facing more fully some of the challenges that they raise. It also recognizes the need of those who preach, teach and train to set those ideas in historical context, including the recent past: how did we get here, how have we learnt from previous work done in this area, and where are there existing resources from which we can continue to benefit? Such resources include those pre-dating the period in the mid-twentieth century in which the set of concerns reviewed in this Introduction about the recognition of the laity in the life of the church comes into focus as a distinct issue.

The approach here is also different from the previous document in some significant respects, as the previous two sections of the Introduction make clear. Rather than simply seeking to present good theology in this area, we are trying to understand why it is that poor theology continues to be evident in our everyday understanding of the church in the world, inhibiting the full participation of all God's people in responding to God's call. Proposals for the healing of our theological vision need to be aligned with the diagnosis that is offered as to what is obscuring it.

In the light of this different aim, we have chosen to address the three themes here in a different order. 'Vocation' is still the focus for the first chapter, but 'ministry' comes next with 'discipleship' being addressed in the final chapter. Debates about 'ministry' are critical for pursuing the diagnosis being offered in the report, as will be evident from some of the examples already given, while 'discipleship' frames the pathways to healing in Christ's company that all members of Christ's body need in order to overcome the obstacles to full participation in his mission and ministry in the world.

We begin with vocation because it provides the crucial context for addressing the first factor identified in the previous section as inhibiting God's people from responding to God's call: a weakness of theological imagination regarding how we fulfil our calling before God day by day in the ordinary experiences of our lives. The chapter introduces an important distinction between three kinds of vocation: relational, social and ministerial. This threefold understanding is then woven through the following two chapters. A significant element in the pathways to healing outlined in the first two chapters concerns the importance of making good distinctions that affirm diverse forms of vocation and ministry, without making one form primary or paradigmatic or letting them fall into a hierarchy of value. The final chapter on discipleship, in contrast, emphasizes what is common to everyone in the life of the church, across these different forms of vocation and ministry, as we respond together to the challenges of receiving God's call. It shows too how the different forms are inseparable from one another.

Although the diagnosis outlined in the previous section is relevant to all three themes, as noted there each chapter has a particular focus on one of the critical factors identified as undermining the consistent affirmation of the participation of all God's people in the whole of God's work. The focuses are on, respectively:

weakness of theological imagination in how we see participation in different areas of society; impoverished understanding of the church; and disorientation in responding to powerful currents within our culture. Correspondingly, the chapter on vocation draws especially on the doctrine of creation, the chapter on ministry on the doctrine of the church, and the chapter on discipleship on the doctrine of Christ, as they seek to point towards pathways to healing, through the renewing of our minds.

Finally, the Faith and Order Commission is well aware that a single report cannot do justice to the many issues that have already been raised in this Introduction. *Kingdom Calling* needs to be read in the context of other work the Commission has been engaged in – not only *Calling All God's People*, but its report on Senior Church Leadership published in 2015, and also *Witness*, which takes the theme of witness as a theological lens for considering the life of Christian communities.[27] The Commission has been giving attention for some time to the subject of missional ecclesiology – the inseparability of church and mission and the implications of this, not least when God's mission is recognized as encompassing the whole world. It is hoped that a publication on this will be forthcoming soon, providing a further and vital resource for addressing the limitations in theological imagination that constrain our freedom to respond together as God's people to God's call.

Chapter 1 Vocation: Being social creatures

Creation, culture and calling

In the beginning: humanity in creation

God's call to humanity begins with creation. To be made in the divine image and likeness is to be called for a purpose, to respond to God's speech to us, by the way we hold responsibilities to God, to one another and to the rest of creation (Gen. 1.26–28; cf. Gen. 2.15–16 & 9.6). All creation begins with God's speaking in Genesis 1, but it is human beings who continue to be called by God in the chapters and books that follow after it in the canon of Scripture and are invited to respond in faith, hope and love. We live in God's world, and wherever we go, God is present, and God is at work, calling us to fulfilment by sharing in that work through our own work in the world. Work in this sense is not limited to what helps secure our livelihood or fulfils a publicly acknowledged role but includes all kinds of purposeful activity. Such work is intrinsic to our creation in the image of God and is inseparable from the making of human societies.[28]

From the beginning, however, the human race has listened to other voices and turned away from God. It belongs to our creation in the divine image that human beings have the capacity to respond to God's address with love and obedience, or with suspicion and disobedience. We have not held fast to the first of these paths and yet our original calling as human creatures remains: to live before God in the time of God's earth, with its days and seasons; to be persons in relation who form families, communities, societies, nations, and networks of international cooperation; and to reflect the divine image in our work, caring for the earth, labouring for life in partnership with other living creatures, and bringing renewal to societies through participation in human cultures that interact with one another in their complex diversity. In the manifold activity that belongs to human beings as creatures made in the divine image, we are to witness to the one God who brought all things into existence and offer our worship, drawing all creation with us into the chorus of God's praise.[29]

In Christ, the original calling of humanity in creation is restored, not taken away in order to be replaced with something superior or less material: to bear the image of God in the world, living under God's reign, and serving as a royal priesthood for creation. For Christ is the one who brings in the reign of God, and in whom all things now hold together. He is the one who has become our great high priest, the saviour of the world. It is in union with him that we can begin to recover our calling to let the image of God shine though the whole of our lives in this world, illuminating the political, social, economic, domestic and cultural environments in which the body of Christ lives and is daily transformed into his likeness by the Holy Spirit's work of sanctification. As one contemporary writer has expressed it, we are called to be

> God's image bearers for the world, and fulfil the mission of being God's image bearers by undertaking the work of culture making.... We are called to an encounter with the life giving God, who imparts transformative grace through the Spirit's empowerment, making it possible to for us to entertain the vocation given to humanity.[30]

Challenges to theological understanding: secularization and individualism

In the outline diagnosis offered in the Introduction for why the Church of England has struggled to uphold the participation of all God's people in all of God's work, a weakness of theological imagination in envisioning the significance of our day-to-day lives within the purposes of God in creation and redemption was identified as the first of three critical factors. Why might it be difficult to sustain the vision of humanity's calling that has just been sketched out, given its deep and strong roots in Scripture and in Scripture's interpretation in Christian tradition? In the Introduction, the effects of secularization in English society over the past century were identified as a crucial part of the context for understanding what is happening here. In order to deepen the diagnosis and begin to outline pathways to healing for our theological imagination, some further exploration of those dynamics is needed.

As was touched on in the Introduction, it has become a commonplace to accept that the origin of the 'modern' world is bound up with secularization, understood as the differentiation of distinct spheres of social existence, with their characteristic institutions. The independence of other spheres from the church and from Christian faith has sometimes been coloured by a stance of bewilderment and scepticism – even hostility – towards traditional sources of self-understanding and authority. Even without that, however, resistance to Christian faith as the guiding lens through which all forms of human endeavour were viewed meant that people learnt to live substantial parts of their lives without any reference to Christ, thereby preparing them over time to live the whole of their lives without any reference to him.[31] That same process of differentiation also undermined both the plausibility and the attractiveness of a thoroughgoing coherence to the whole of life, such as is offered by Christian faith. Although the appeal of such coherence continues to linger, abstract values are more likely to be upheld as underpinning consistency across the various spheres. For example, a just culture – instead of being conceived in terms of what God has revealed – has become closely associated with the terms 'equality and diversity'. Instead of coherence being provided for human equality by God's creative act and the different ways of living a human life as responses to God's redemptive call, political values abstracted from this narrative offer a new vision to the imagination. These values do not remain abstract, however, but populate institutional life, making themselves visible but occluding the Christian story. To respond to that by offering instead a vision of life's coherence based on doctrinal truths might seem at best superfluous, at worst distorting or antisocial.

Alongside this dynamic of differentiation, the pervasive influence of a multi-stranded individualism is also relevant here: the idea that we exist fundamentally as separate individuals from one another, whose nature is to seek our own pleasure, exercise our own free will and express our own unique selfhood.[32] While some elements of this picture may have points of contact with a Christian perspective, it stands in evident contrast with the theological approach sketched out earlier in this chapter that sees human beings as persons in relation, constituted in and by their relations rather than finally independent from them:

> We are made in the image of the God of love, whose very being is a communion of love, and who we are is found in our own belonging in that communion of love. Our identity as human beings is never as atomized, isolated individuals. We are who we are because we are forged and framed out of relationship, from our very first coming into being through the mutual self-giving of our mothers and fathers.[33]

That is not to say that the individualism that pervades much of our culture accords no value to relationships, but it will always be liable to see them as secondary to the autonomous individual, to be valued for the extent to which they enable the individual to pursue their own pleasure, achieve their own freedom or express their own uniqueness. That tends to place the weight on relationships that individuals are perceived as able to shape for themselves: family, friendship, romantic love. It is here that freedom and the meaning it enables are to be found, by contrast with the 'given' texture of social relations encountered in institutions and associated forms of authority, which appear as external constraints. Much has been written over the past hundred years in philosophy and social science as well as theology that brings this to the fore, yet the picture of the self-sufficient individual existing outside of and prior to society and culture has proved remarkably tenacious.[34]

As will be considered further in the next section, Christians today are likely to feel far less confident than their predecessors from even a hundred years ago about seeing human society and culture as part of God's creation. Moreover, widely-shared assumptions about these may mean they do not readily regard social and cultural life as integral to humanity's fulfilment of God's first commandment in Genesis to fill the earth and to how human beings respond to God's calling in creation. The differentiation of social space and privatization of religion associated with secularization contribute to such difficulties, as already discussed. Beyond those factors, the individualism that marks our culture encourages us to shrink the zone of theological significance to the drama of the individual soul before God, to individual acts of moral goodness or evil and to the fellowship of the church as a community of those who choose one another to be companions and supporters. Once we fall into assuming that while 'individual' human beings are valued elements of God's creation, our social and cultural life is no more than a contingent product of human history, then we start to give up on the relevance of theology to understanding what is actually constitutive for us as beings created by God to live on God's earth. We circumscribe the spiritual within the privatized zones of individual religious practice and discrete religious institutions, both of which are kept carefully fenced off from the common spaces of public life.

Creation and kingdom

By way of a pathway towards healing, we need to sustain a theological imagination that embraces the whole of our lives within the sweep of God's creation: yes, marred by sin to an extent we can only barely comprehend, yet insofar as institutions, cultural artefacts, economic life etc. remain forms of persons in relation, also encompassed by the redeeming work of Christ, to be transformed by the reign of God on earth. Our doctrine of creation needs to underpin our resistance to the message that Christian doctrine is essentially irrelevant to ordinary participation in society and culture. In this way, a vision can be renewed of a coherent human life, made so by Christ in whom all things hold together.

As it came to be expressed by Christian writers of the early centuries, the church is no more and no less than 'the world, reconciled': of course it can also be described sociologically as one specialized set of institutions alongside others, but theologically the church is humanity set free by faith in Christ to live in anticipation of the fulfilment of God's purposes for all creation.[35] As such, the church is the foretaste of the whole of human life united in the reign of God, and as human life is intrinsically social life, life in society, the drawing near of the kingdom that Jesus announced from the outset of his ministry must mean restoration of the people of God under the rule of God. Christ's proclamation of the good news of the kingdom of the one who is creator of all is inseparable from the transforming unity in his body of all peoples, every society and every culture. Anglican tradition has stressed the character of the church as itself 'an outward, visible, and united society' expressing the communion of all humanity in God through the saving work of Christ.[36]

God's calling of the church, therefore, is inseparable from God's calling of humanity in creation. God set human beings, as social and cultural creatures, at the heart of creation with a purpose in and for that creation, and God has not abandoned humanity or the purpose that is bound up with it. To sustain that purpose and maintain a witness to what the whole of humanity is called to become, 'The Church is in Christ like a sacrament or as a sign and instrument both of a very closely knit union with God and of the unity of the whole human race.'[37] The unity of the church should therefore encompass the fullness of humanity in its creaturely diversity, called in the beginning to be fruitful and to fill the earth, generating the rich and continually growing tapestry of cultures that meet together before God in the church's witness and worship. A need to overcome impoverishment in our understanding of the church was the second factor identified in the diagnosis offered in the Introduction, and the next chapter will focus on this at greater length.

Distinguishing different vocations

Clarifying terms: calling and vocation

God calls humanity, God calls a people for the sake of all people, and God calls each one of us. Indeed, at critical points in the scriptural story, the faithfulness of the community to its calling hinges upon an individual being faithful to his or her calling, as we see in different ways with Abraham, Moses and Elijah, with Mary, the Twelve and Paul, and supremely in Jesus himself. That is not to minimize the extent to which a call may lead to isolation and rejection for the individual who responds faithfully from the community that is failing in faithfulness, such as Jesus experienced, following Israel's prophets before him, not least Jeremiah.

In the Gospels, we see people responding to God's call in Christ in different ways, as Jesus asks different things of them. Within the Gospels, some are called to leave behind homes, families and livelihoods in order to accompany him in his ministry. Some remain where they are and provide places to stay for him and those accompanying him, welcoming his transforming presence into the midst of their continuing routines. Others are explicitly told not to travel with him but to go back to their homes and share the good news there, such as the man healed of demon possession in the country of the Gerasenes (Mark 5.1–20). Paul stresses in his description of the church as Christ's body that each of us receives gifts from God, and none should be singled out as intrinsically superior to others (Rom. 12.3–8; 1 Cor. 12.4–31). Similarly, the varied range of callings for those who follow Christ today should not be turned into a hierarchy but rather affirmed and celebrated.

In responding to God's call and finding our place among God's people, we accept commitments that mark us in deep and lasting ways. We can refer to acceptance of such life-shaping commitment as a vocation that we receive from God that enables us to serve others and contribute with them to the common good. Thus understood, a vocation is one way in which we may live out our calling as human persons and members of Christ's body.

Thus vocation finds its bearings in the dialogue between God and humanity that flows from the saving work of Christ; this is how the word is used in this report. Inevitably, that brings some tension with the influence of individualism as noted in the previous section, which encourages us to think of life-shaping commitments as matters for individuals to choose for themselves based on what will be most conducive to their self-fulfilment. The doctrine of creation, in profound contrast, teaches us that we are God's handiwork, redeemed through Christ to fulfil the purposes for which we were made: 'For we are what he has made us, created in Christ Jesus for good works, which God prepared beforehand to be our way of life' (Eph. 2.10). Vocation is then always response to another, and it concerns both the discovery of what has been given to us as well as the exploration of what may unfold before us. It is inseparable from recognizing and embracing the truth of our being as creatures called to glorify the divine creator in the specific circumstances of our lives, which include the relations with which our reality as persons is interwoven – intimate, social and ecclesial relations.

Vocation as it is being presented here forms a crucial part of how we respond to God's call, for all who are able to consider commitments of this kind. Characterized in this way, vocation is a theological and spiritual category that is relevant across many different situations and circumstances. There is a challenge here for people within those groups that have tended to regard vocation as their special territory, including clergy, but also to those outside those groups who may have felt happy to leave others to grapple with the demands that follow from framing our commitments as response to God's address and not just a matter of our own private choice. Recovering a sense of vocation that opens it up to the whole people of God and recognizes its variety in terms of both focus and duration, without rendering it nebulous or muddled, is a vital part of the healing needed to address the weakness of theological imagination regarding everyday life identified in the initial diagnosis.

To say that vocation is relevant for all kinds of Christians is not the same as saying that it covers the whole of Christian life. Not everything we do in faithfulness to God's call will form part of a life-shaping commitment: there are likely to be times when we act in obedience to God in ways that do not readily fit within the pattern of a settled vocation. Vocation is about what gives continuity and distinguishing shape to our unfolding journey of discipleship.

As will be explored more fully in the following section, vocation does not depend on a heavenly voice suddenly directing us to do something out of the ordinary. It is rather a matter of thinking and praying about the life-shaping commitments by which we serve others and contribute to the common good within the creation which we share together – the ones we have already made and the new ones we might make in the future. It involves asking: can I discern here a way of life to which God is calling me, and can I therefore understand my commitment to it as the receiving of a vocation from God?

Three types of vocation: social, relational, ministerial

Vocations as thus understood can be of different kinds, and we may have more than one at a time, as Luther made clear.[38] Christians have used the language of vocation to talk about three intersecting areas in particular: social roles, forms of close relationship, and the ministries by which some serve others within the body of Christ. In the case of each of these areas, participation in them is something that pertains to all Christians throughout our lives as part of our common calling: as human beings who have been redeemed in Christ, we are all called to contribute to the common good of society, to sustain relationships of love and mutual belonging, and to share in the ministry of the church as the company of those baptized into Christ's body (a subject that will be discussed further in the next chapter). For some Christians, some of the time, however, that share in the common calling to life in society, to close relationships and to the ministry of the church will find expression in a particular form of life-shaping commitment, entered into as part of the obedience of discipleship. Accepting in response to God's call a commitment to a specific occupation, profession or sphere of work, to share in God's work in God's world, becomes a vocation. So does accepting a commitment to another person in marriage and family life, or to a religious community or to celibacy. So does accepting a commitment to serve the church in a lifelong ministry, or in a specific place.

We should, then, make a distinction between *social vocations, relational vocations and ministerial vocations* in the Christian life.[39] Vocation in this sense is about how the calling of all God's people takes on a specific shape, with specific limitations and freedoms, in the lives of different people. How these vocations relate to one another will be an important theme in this report, so it will be helpful to rehearse briefly some of the ways in which they have been understood through Christian history.

The Middle Ages as a period in Western church history are marked by the centrality of one kind of relational vocation: vocation to the religious life. While it took increasingly varied form in later centuries, it remained broadly defined by accepting disciplines of poverty, chastity and obedience. In this period, the language of calling becomes closely associated with the religious life, as the paradigmatic form of whole-hearted response to the call of discipleship. Especially after clerical celibacy became the required norm, it overlapped to some extent with the ministerial vocation to priesthood, which nonetheless also provided something of a counterpoint because of its pastoral character.

That shifted significantly in mid-twentieth century Catholic thought. Since the later Middle Ages, the term 'evangelical counsels' had been used to refer to the vows of poverty, chastity and obedience that defined the consecrated life: a life separated from, and by definition not accessible to, the vast majority of Christians. The implication was that the 'gospel' life could be lived by those under religious vows in a way that was not possible for the lay faithful. Across various documents of the Second Vatican Council, however, there is a profound refocusing of traditional teaching. Rather than the vows defining what discipleship means, the Council wanted discipleship to illuminate what the vows mean: the intentional shaping of a way of life in which Christians are free to follow in the way of the Son of God, which is the way of love for God and neighbour that leads to ever deepening union with the one who became incarnate in Christ for our salvation.[40] The focus on discipleship as growing in love enables the Council texts to embed their teaching about contemporary discipleship in the broad, deep stream of Catholic tradition, while also opening up a reading of poverty, chastity and obedience as attitudes of the heart that need not be confined to those in religious orders, but rather pertain to anyone who would say yes to the call: 'Follow me.' [41]

That way of understanding the 'evangelical counsels' also enabled the renewed affirmation of marriage and family life as a relational vocation alongside that of priests and religious. This theme was explored by Hans Urs von Balthasar, one of the most influential Roman Catholic theologians in the second half of the twentieth century. According to him, there is 'a baptismal call to the family of the Church, then to a particular state within the Church, and finally to a concrete situation within a particular state.'[42] For von Balthasar, there are essentially two 'particular' states within the church: the secular state, which includes and is to some extent defined by marriage, and the 'state of election', which embraces priesthood and religious life. The notion of marriage as a vocation within the life of the Church is striking, not least because it cuts against two common assumptions: first, that marriage is the 'default setting' for Christians, and second, that marriage is about two individuals making their own choices without reference to others. This emerging understanding of marriage as vocation within Roman Catholicism recalls the teaching of Luther and other Protestant Reformers and finds a clear parallel in the affirmation of the 1958 Lambeth Conference that 'marriage is a vocation to holiness, through which men and women share in the love and creative purpose of God.'[43] *Living in Love and Faith*, due to be published by the Church of England's House of Bishops soon after the release of this report, is expected to affirm the parallel claim that celibacy can be integral to a person's vocation, i.e. there are relational vocations other than marriage.[44]

The Protestant Reformers of the sixteenth century sharply challenged medieval Catholicism's close association of calling with the religious life and with priesthood as similarly requiring celibacy and separation from ordinary work. There is a radical tone to many of their pronouncements on this. Luther wrote that 'all Christians are truly of spiritual status, and there is no difference among them except that of office.'[45] As well as abolishing the requirement of clerical celibacy and seeking to bring to an end the mentalities along with the institutions that sustained the religious life, they highlighted what we are referring to as social vocation as applicable to the whole church, thereby releasing the concept of vocation from confinement only to clergy and those under religious vows.[46] This was an important recovery of the presentation of work from the opening chapters of the Bible, beginning with agriculture, as intrinsic to the human calling in creation, including the counterpoint of work and rest that becomes woven into the life of God's people at Mount Sinai as an expression of our being made in the image of the one who also works and rests in bringing this world to be. Many of the Reformers were concerned to enable communities to share in a Christian sabbath of rest from labour, as the proper accompaniment to opening people's eyes to the dignity of their work as response to divine call. Work is an integral part of human life in creaturely time, but within the rhythm of work and rest, through the whole of which God is acknowledged and glorified.

The Reformers believed that every Christian should understand themselves as called by God to a role within society as a way of serving others and contributing to the common good. Such vocations included the calling to domestic roles as well as other forms of occupation, thereby encompassing what is here being termed relational as well as social forms of vocation. Underpinning this was an appreciation of work of all kinds as belonging within God's purposes for humanity in creation that can be traced back through earlier Christian tradition, against the classical ideal of release from labour as the condition for the fulfilment of human life.[47] That did not mean ignoring either the effects of the Fall on economic life, as signalled in Genesis 3.17–19, or the realities of constant repetition and exhausting physical demand involved in many occupations. Nonetheless, through intentional, diverse, cooperative action for the common good, human beings express in their appointed way the image of the one who made the world.

In the Church of England's Book of Common Prayer (1662), the Second Collect for Good Friday articulates this very clearly, in a way that expresses the expectation that Christians normally find God's calling for them in their daily occupations:

> Almighty and everlasting God, by whose Spirit the whole body of the Church is governed and sanctified: Receive our supplications and prayers, which we offer before thee for all estates of men in thy holy Church, that every member of the same, in his vocation and ministry, may truly and godly serve thee; through our Lord and Saviour Jesus Christ. Amen.

This revolutionary approach to Christian vocation is also attested in other texts from the Church of England's historic formularies, such as the Catechism in the Book of Common Prayer.[48] Yet this powerful affirmation of social vocation has not been easy to sustain over the centuries. For instance, although the Collect just cited finds a continuing place in modern language form in Common Worship, some subtle changes might be observed. For instance, 'for all your faithful people' replaces 'for all estates of men in thy holy church'; while is not easy to propose a precise contemporary equivalent for 'estates', it conveyed an explicit reference to the make-up of society – not just the church – which is obscured in the Common Worship version. Similarly, the Collect's appearance in the provision for 'Ministry (including Ember Days)', historically associated with ordinations, makes it natural to read the phrase 'vocation and ministry' as referring mainly if not exclusively to ministerial vocations (in the terminology used here) and not to social vocations at all.[49] Part of the long-term context for this report is the way that ministerial vocations have come to eclipse both relational and social vocations in the post-Reformation Church of England, a development that accelerates with the pace of social change from the nineteenth century onwards and the associated pressures of modernity. It must be admitted that such liturgical changes have not hindered but arguably have hastened this tendency.

Social vocation in a post-Christendom society

There are various factors that have led churches to be more hesitant in affirming social vocations than were the Reformers of the sixteenth century. At that time, apart from the small number of Christians associated with what is sometimes called the Radical Reformation, the value of Christendom as the prevailing condition in Western Europe was taken for granted, i.e. a society in which a Christian church was favoured by the state, whose leaders were members of that church and gave it comprehensive formal and informal · influence in political and cultural life. Such a society understood itself to be fundamentally Christian, ordered in a way that fitted with Christian faith. By contrast, England today might be considered to be a post-Christendom society, meaning one in which this self-understanding is no longer the norm, although the legacy of Christendom continue to be evident in certain respects, not just in institutions such as the role of bishops in the House of Lords or the Church of England's distinctive presence in education, hospitals and prisons, but in the sense of affiliation with the Church of England on the part of many who do not regularly participate in church life.

We will need to return to this idea of post-Christendom in subsequent chapters, but its relevance for the current discussion is that we are unlikely to have the same level of confidence as our sixteenth-century predecessors that every lawful occupation within our society can be a fruitful place for living out a vocation from God. Luther had argued that a Christian could even be called to the job of executioner; this could be contrasted with the pre-Christendom era, when consideration of which occupations were compatible with Christian life was a normal part of the preparation for candidates for baptism. In the contemporary context, there may also be questions that Christians want to consider with the help of others if they believe themselves called to be, for example, debt collectors, military interrogators, certain kinds of fertility specialist, or certain kinds of fund manager, precisely because such lines of work might, at least if carried out in certain ways, fail to represent the kingdom of God. Those questions, explored together with others, may nonetheless receive satisfyingly godly answers – in terms perhaps of the service of justice, the prevention of crime/the preservation of peace, the fulfilment of the creation mandate or economic stewardship.

The Reformers' advocacy of social vocation rested on a strong doctrine of providence combined with an expectation of relative stability in social roles: my work and place within society, which I can reasonably expect to maintain over the majority of my lifetime, is not merely a combined product of chance and choice, but expresses, in however qualified a way, the purposes of God. In the contemporary social context, to be able to accept one's paid work as a vocation, understood as a 'form of life-shaping commitment taken up in response to God's call that enables us to serve others and contribute to the common good' (to use the formulation given earlier), might appear as something of a luxury. It might be denied, for instance, to those who find themselves unemployed against their will, or shuttling between short-term or zero-hours contracts, or holding multiple jobs at the same time for different organizations with which any contractual relationship is weak at best. Commitment to one type of occupation or profession, in such contexts, does not look like a possibility that is truly available. In this respect too, we struggle to share the Reformers' confidence that every adult Christian is able to receive and live out a social vocation in their current circumstances.

Although the focus of the discussion so far has been on paid occupations, social vocation is by no means limited to that. Caring for a child or elderly relative or maintaining a home for others to enjoy may also be a full-time occupation that becomes a social vocation, without any financial remuneration. Decisions about unpaid roles may be as critical for responding faithfully to God's call in society as decisions about profession, career and paid work. Volunteering is a key dimension of contemporary civic society about which the church should be energetic and celebratory rather than embarrassed in the face of the challenges as well as the opportunities. A reliance on volunteers characterizes all high-cost social enterprises, as anyone who has to do with hospitals and schools will know. This is also true of the church, and indeed it is one element in the concern to maximize the contribution of lay people.

There was a remarkable attempt to recover the emphasis of the Anglican Reformers on social vocation in the Board of Education report from 1985, *All are Called*, referred to in the Introduction:

> Because all human beings are made in the image of God, they are called to become the People of God, the Church, servants and ministers and citizens of the Kingdom, a new humanity in Jesus Christ. Though we are tainted by our sinfulness, God's wonderful grace and love offer us all this common Christian vocation....

> We are all called no matter what our occupations may be. There is no special status in the Kingdom for those in 'top jobs' or 'important responsibilities'. Cleaners and car dealers are called just as much as professors and lawyers and missionary nurses. And unemployed people and redundant people and 'unemployable' people are called just like everybody else. Our human dignity does not depend on having a job.

> Nor does our calling – our vocation – depend on any kind of ordination. There are still many deep controversies about what ordination may signify, in many Churches and within our own Church

of England. But it certainly does not indicate any special 'grade' of Christian, more holy than the laity. And for everybody, bishops, priests and laity together, the great sacrament of our common calling is our baptism, which signifies our glorious new life in Christ.[50]

There is, on the one hand, much here that the Church of England today could and should still affirm. That includes the centrality of baptism for the theology of calling and vocation, a theme to which we will need to return in both the following two chapters. The refusal to accord higher status to characteristically middle-class occupations and to professional roles requiring university education remains a much-needed corrective to assumptions that are difficult to shift, though the sudden re-evaluation of the jobs of 'key workers' during the coronavirus pandemic has been helpful in this respect: 'Cleaners and car dealers are called just as much as professors and lawyers and missionary nurses.' The insistence that calling and vocation are relevant for the whole people of God, and not just those who are ordained, is wholly in accord with the central message of this chapter.

On the other hand, some questions are also raised by the passage. As noted already, it is possible that asking questions about the 'fit' between my present occupation and our common calling in baptism might lead me to conclude that I am actually *not* called to continue in the occupation in which I find myself. What does it mean to live with the tension of believing that what I am doing is not my vocation but feeling powerless to change that situation? That tension would also apply to those who feel the absence of work that might be grasped as vocation: 'unemployed people and redundant people and "unemployable" people are called just like everybody else. Our human dignity does not depend on having a job.' Yet what they are called to is not immediately evident, and while human dignity does not depend on having a job it includes the freedom to undertake work as purposeful activity in the world.[51]

What is the role of the church, then, in both interpreting and addressing the situation of those who do not experience their current circumstances as corresponding with their vocation as response to God's call? In the case of social vocations, that may involve identifying temptations and besetting sins, but also structural injustice and practices that undermine human dignity, including discrimination that makes unjustified assumptions about what roles will or will not fit people in a particular category. There will be a need for discernment, sometimes under acute pressure, as to what response the person should make: is it to seek change and reform through continued participation in the situation, or to step away from it, perhaps to advocate for wider changes within the social context?[52] Without undermining the responsibility of each person to grapple with such vocational questions, the importance of addressing them with the church should be affirmed.

To do that means thinking theologically about society, and the institutions and forces that shape it. Anglicans have a rich tradition of social theology to draw on as a resource here.[53] They can also benefit from interaction with other traditions, notably Catholic Social Teaching. One idea that may be helpful here is that of 'vocational responsibility' – that different institutions within society, such as businesses, schools, hospitals and the judiciary, have distinct and divinely-given callings, with the state itself having a calling to hold the various institutions together and enable them to foster the common good of the whole of society. Such a perspective affirms the distinctiveness of different institutions while resisting the claim that modernity means their autonomy and independence from accountability to God or indeed to an overarching conception of the common good.

If the calling of institutions within society is to provide certain social goods, then it becomes possible to understand the social vocations of individuals as characteristically consisting in a call to help a given institution fulfil its calling under God within society. Just as with relational and ministerial vocations, social vocations are lived out with others and therefore need to be in various ways shared and negotiated with others, as well as tested by them. It also becomes possible to identify an ethical framework for that institution's life within which it is possible to open up an ethical critique of the way that it currently happens to be operating; indeed, articulating such a critique might be an integral part of the social vocation of a Christian called to serve Christ in the context of that institution. Here again the question arises of how those facing such a challenge in their social vocation are supported as part of the body of Christ, and indeed connected with others who may be struggling with the same challenge or one relating closely to it.

One of the lessons to be learnt from the review of church history in this section is that it has always been difficult to maintain attention to the diversity of callings in the life of the church without ignoring some altogether, or implying that there is a definite ranking, in which one or two are superior to others. There is an inevitable but regrettable tendency for the language of vocation in the church to gravitate towards certain forms of life rather than others. At different times and in different places, it has been expected that those answering positively the question 'Is God calling you?' are likely to e.g. enter the religious life, or become ordained ministers, or offer themselves for missionary service abroad. Some of the ongoing conversations within the contemporary Church of England that lie behind this report have been about the continuing association between vocation as response to God's call and ministerial vocation as either its sole or its primary expression. As has been seen earlier in this section of the chapter, such concerns have roots reaching far back in Christian history, and to address them requires careful attention and indeed a certain discipline in the way that those who hold pastoral and teaching responsibility in the church speak about vocation: discipline in ensuring it is spoken about as a normal part of Christian discipleship, and careful attention in fostering a rich understanding of it that encompasses relational, social and ministerial vocations and values the diversity within each of those categories.

For the sake of healing our theological imagination regarding everyday life in society, it therefore seems critically important that the term 'vocation' when used in an unqualified way *always* has space to include relational and social as well as ministerial vocations. When its meaning is articulated, these different possibilities need to be explicitly acknowledged. It is also vital to make clear that it is entirely common for members of the church is to hold two or three of these kinds of vocation together – to let one's life be shaped in response to God's call by a vocation to a specific pattern of relationship, a vocation to a certain role within society, and a vocation to a form of ministry as service offered to some by others in the church. At the same time, it should also be acknowledged that the 'weight' of vocation will be felt in many cases as falling on one or two of these, rather than equally on all three. Moreover, many and perhaps most Christians will have the experience at some point of feeling that their vocation in one at least of these spheres is being denied or frustrated, or that there is an uncomfortable tension between them. That may prompt important questions about vocational discernment, to which further attention is given in the next section.

Discernment, conviction, choice and obedience

The process of discernment

Discernment will be a familiar term for anyone who has sought to explore a call to ordained, licensed or authorized ministry in the Church of England; indeed, such exploration is often referred to institutionally as 'the discernment process'. Two critical assumptions are likely to shape the way that this process unfolds. They might be summarized as follows:

● discernment involves not just the individual member of the church but also the church as a body seeking to know what is right for the individual concerned, with the individual expected to understand and attend to the concerns and priorities of the whole body in this process;

● vocation is normally accompanied by an interior conviction on the part of the individual that this is the path God wants them to follow, a conviction which unfolds over time, is confirmed by interaction with others in the church, and can be coherently narrated by the individual concerned.

An immediate challenge for sustaining a proper sense of the variety of vocations without creating an implicit hierarchy is that in the case of social vocations there is no obvious parallel for these common assumptions. Should there be? In this section of the chapter, the case will be made for an ecclesial dimension of discernment for social vocations. But what about the second of these two assumptions, which might be summarized as the presence of narratable interior conviction? In considering a calling to be a scientist, farmer or carer, is this to be expected or is it sufficient and indeed normal to say: this is a role that is needed within the life of society as part of God's purposes for humanity, I have the capacity to fulfil that role, and therefore I will do it as a disciple of Jesus Christ who is seeking the kingdom of God?

Even in the context of ministerial vocations, the level of investment by the church in the process of discernment may not be the same in all cases. In the Church of England, for instance, national common standards for discernment of ordained ministry do not apply in the same way to licensed lay ministries, where practices may vary significantly across dioceses. The process of discernment may be more minimal still for authorized lay ministries, and perhaps close to non-existent for recognized lay ministries, especially where parishes are desperate to plug gaps in support for current activities.

Does the varying length and intensity of the discernment process reflect the value the church accords to different vocations? That should not and need not be the case: as vocations vary, so will the appropriate process of discernment that prepares for them. Yet it is reasonable to expect that there will be some provision for vocational discernment wherever the church wishes to speak in earnest about vocation.

Interior conviction as criterion for discernment

The assumption that interior conviction is needed at least for some kinds of discernment has not always been present within the church, for vocations of any kind. The identification of specific criteria for those being considered for positions of responsibility in the church begins within the documents of the New Testament (Acts 6.1–6; 1 Tim. 3.1–13; Titus 1.5–9), but we find nothing there about an inner sense of calling to such a position. In fact, early Christian history provides many examples of devout people initially resisting the ordination for which they had been chosen by the congregation without being consulted, and then accepting it as a service needed for the good of the church; the initiative in discernment is here clearly with the church and not the individual, nor is there any expectation that the person 'feels' called.

Likewise, in writings of the fourth and fifth centuries urging the embrace of the monastic life, it is a matter of responding to the universal call of God to fulfil the divine commandments and thereby save your soul, not of detecting some inner movement. Those who enter the monastic life choose the safest way of saying yes to God, and the one that is perceived to enable the most complete response. In the thirteenth century, the position of Thomas Aquinas remained essentially the same.[54] All should be encouraged to consider a call to the religious life, and anyone expressing a willingness to enter it should be encouraged to pursue it. There is no need to engage in introspection about the existence of an inner 'feeling' of calling: Christ invites all to the path of discipleship, the religious life is the safest and best way to follow it, and God will give the grace needed to those who choose to take it. Aquinas was aware that some people were moved by 'charity' to seek the religious life: admirable as that was, it was not required.

The notion that evidence of interior conviction is needed to authenticate a calling in the life of the church only begins to emerge clearly in sixteenth-century Roman Catholicism, being particularly associated with Ignatius Loyola and the Jesuits. It might be noted that while Ignatius himself was keen to promote vocations to priesthood and the religious life, the use of the 'Spiritual Exercises' as a tool for discernment is perfectly applicable also to social vocations. The aim here is to clarify what the voice of Christ is saying: his summons comes to us, as to those who once followed him in Galilee, as a word of command that invites immediate obedience, but there remains a need for deliberation, individual and shared, as to the form that obedience should take. Moreover, the manifold workings of sin mean that we are easily confused, distracted and mistaken as to what Christ is calling us to do. Those same workings of sin may also mean that our obedient 'yes' to Christ at one moment may be undermined over months and years by persisting sinful habits of motivation and behaviour, so there is a need to open space for continual transformation of our hearts and minds by the indwelling of the Holy Spirit if we are to respond fully to God's call. These insights into discernment and vocation have been developed over the following centuries to become a resource for Christians across denominational boundaries that is clearly applicable to social, relational and ministerial vocations alike.[55]

It might be helpful to frame this kind of discernment in the context of reflecting on the 'fit' between my current circumstances and the commitment God may be asking me to accept as a vocation. It may be that I have become too comfortable in accepting that lack of fit, or that I lack courage to embrace a new commitment, or that I am simply unsure what it is that God is asking of me. The kind of exploration that the 'Spiritual Exercises' helped to frame can evidently be of value in such cases. Nonetheless, it is certainly not necessary to go through such a process and discover some element of narratable interior conviction in order to accept a life-shaping commitment of the kind we have been describing as a vocation from God. The primary vocational discernment concerns rather the judgment that the character of this commitment is in accord with the common calling of the church in baptism, that I have the capacity to fulfil it, and that in so doing I can fruitfully serve others and contribute with them to the common good. The responsibility for making that judgment will normally be shared between the person discerning the calling, those who would be involved in living out the commitment and the church as a community of wisdom about faithful living before God.

Supporting and testing discernment

It follows from recognising the importance of exercising vocational discernment with regard to social role and pattern of relationships for the sake of conformity to Christ that the challenges of such discernment should routinely be the subject of preaching and teaching. Particular attention needs to be paid to those who are at stages of life where formative choices about commitments in these spheres are likely to be made. Support for young people is clearly especially crucial here, underlining the importance of investment in church youth work and student ministries and training for those involved that equips them to foster the process of discernment about all three types of vocation. Questions about how to live out long-standing commitments, when it is time to lay some down and when it is time to take on new ones are also likely to recur at regular intervals throughout a lifetime of discipleship. They may arise at points of transition and change in responsibilities, such as retirement, welcoming a new child into the family, or adjusting to the departure of grown-up children from the family home.[56]

Encouragement, then, should be given through regular preaching and teaching for all to attend to discernment of vocation, with indication of the opportunities that exist for focused conversation and counsel to assist this, such as mentoring, spiritual accompaniment and periods of retreat. As noted in the previous section, that needs to include reflection on the difficulty some may experience in living out social or other kinds of vocation, not just because of inner resistance but also because of barriers in society, including prejudice and discrimination. The capacity to assist the baptized with discernment of social and relational as well as ministerial vocations should be a normal part of the pastoral ministry of Christian communities. Although many examples could be given where there is such capacity, research suggests there is significant scope for building up engagement by local churches in this area.[57]

Discernment of vocation always involves some element of testing, as a person's willingness to take on a life-shaping commitment that enables them to serve others and contribute to the common good needs to be recognized and accepted by the people to whom it would most immediately commit them. Again, this will take different forms with different vocations. As noted earlier, there are formal processes in the Church of England for testing of ministerial vocations. With social vocations, it might be in part through professional exams, job interviews, apprenticeships or work experience. With relational vocations, it hinges on mutual agreement to share a common life, within marriage as within religious community. The sense that the magnitude of the commitments involved needs time to be tested out is expressed in different ways by the period of engagement on the one hand and the novitiate on the other.

Vocation and choice

The process of discernment presupposes the action of choice: the call of Christ comes as an invitation to which a response must be made – the choice to say yes and follow him, or the choice to say no and walk away. This way of framing vocational discernment faces some challenges in the contemporary context. One comes from the ideology of choosing as the way in which a person finds and asserts identity, within the dominant cultural paradigm of what the philosopher Charles Taylor has called 'expressive individualism'.[58] Choice here becomes an autonomous and self-creating action, rather than a response to the call of another. It is easy in our culture for discernment of the call of Christ by attending to interior currents of feeling and conviction to blur into responses to the rather different summons to self-actualization and self-fulfilment. A consistent understanding that vocation is received from God to enable us to serve others and contribute with them to the common good is crucial here: it is a way of finding our place under God's guidance in relation to others, not independently from them. Vocation is never only or even primarily for my sake separately from other human beings: that is why testing of vocation by and with others, however challenging and indeed painful it may sometimes be, should not be resented or simply bypassed because of the strength of a personal conviction.

At the same time, because a vocation is received from God, to discern it is to recognize that which has been given to us at God's hand, as a duty that constrains us and not just as one thing among a range of options available for us to pick as we will. Indeed, for some there may be a very strong sense of vocation as accepting what has been laid upon them, as a way of living out their response to God's call. That would be true of many, for instance, whose lives are profoundly shaped by commitments to care for family members who have long-term needs for constant support.[59]

For some, however, choosing to accept a vocation may be obstructed by the actions of others and by structural features of the social order, as was mentioned earlier when discussing social vocations. Racism, individual and institutional, and other forms of injustice are opposed to the flourishing of the diversity of human vocations, and they have marred the life of the church as well as other parts of society. The range of commitments available to some may be severely constrained by their circumstances, especially those who suffer from oppression and marginalization. In perhaps an increasing number of paid occupations, there is no obvious path of career progression, and considerable uncertainty about permanence. While Christians today may still want to say with George Herbert that the service of Christ 'makes drudgery divine', they will also want to advocate for a society in which there is good work for all, informed by their understanding of human society and culture as part of God's good creation that has been distorted by sin.

We also need to remain mindful of the experience of those whose lives are marked by frustration that what they believe they are called to choose in faithfulness to Christ does not seem to be possible to live out. What of those who become convinced of a vocation to marriage that ends in divorce, to a form of work that terminates with redundancy, or to a ministry that the church does not open to them? In such cases there will be a need to lament what has been lost, but also to explore the extent to which the vocation either remains yet should take different form or should be laid aside to make space for new ways of responding to Christ's call, for he does not cease to address us.

Challenges for vocation

This chapter has argued that fostering an understanding of vocation that embraces social, relational and ministerial vocations is vital for healing our theological vision of how God is at work in all creation.

To do that, we face significant challenges.

- We easily slip into thinking that a vocation from God is something that only applies to a minority of Christians. That means vocation gets used to make some feel special if not spiritually superior, while others assume that there is no need for them to think and pray about God's call when considering significant life commitments. Both are damaging perspectives to adopt. This has to change.

- Valuing social and relational vocations is critical if we are to uphold an understanding of human persons as created by God for relationships in society. We have, however, inherited the habit of talking about 'vocations' in a church context as if that can only mean becoming a minister, and possibly a monk / nun or a missionary as well. If we are going to change the way we think about God's purposes in society, we need to get serious about social vocations. To do that, we will have to watch the way we talk about vocation and learn some new habits of thinking and speaking.

- Vocation is not something we are meant to figure out by ourselves. Church communities should be places where questions about social, relational and ministerial vocations are regularly raised in preaching and teaching and can be considered in safe and trusted settings, as a normal part of church life. It does not matter whether the word 'vocation' is always used. But if that is to happen, the culture of our church communities will in many cases need to shift.

- Such exploration of vocation within church communities needs to include space for listening to those who feel frustrated in seeking to respond to God's call and for reflecting on those factors that limit people's scope for living out vocation, including discrimination and other forms of injustice. Vocation always concerns how we can contribute to the common good, not just our private self-fulfilment. A church that wants to talk seriously about vocation therefore needs to be ready to talk seriously about social theology, that is, a theological understanding of our social reality that addresses questions of what is good, right, and just.

Chapter 2 Ministry: Understanding the Church

The trouble with ministry

It is no accident that the concern repeatedly voiced over the past seven decades regarding lack of support for the participation of the whole people of God in the whole work of God has found particularly sharp expression in frustration around ministry. Some of that frustration relates to the potential tension between the two perceived imperatives for the church in a post-Christendom context marked by the dynamics of secularization in shaping priorities for the laity, as described in the Introduction. The first imperative, to address the weakening of Christian influence in society, was associated with a focus on lay discipleship. The second, to deal with the decline in numbers and resources for the institutional church, was associated with a focus on lay ministry. Those preoccupied with the second may be likely to think that issues around ministry (of all kinds) are the overriding priority, leaving those concerned with the first fearing a lack of commitment to sustaining the church's witness to the nation as a whole.

In exploring that tension further, however, questions also emerge regarding the relationship between ordained and other forms of ministry, as was also noted in the Introduction. To what extent are these other forms only supplementary to ordained ministry, with the implication that this is fundamental to the life of the church in a way that they are not? Is their growth in recent history ultimately a pragmatic response to decline in numbers of ordained ministers, or a proper expression of the abundance of Christ's gifts to his church? Are lay ministries always to be exercised under the authority of ordained ministers, assisting them and working under their direction?

The second and third main sections of this chapter tackle these questions, developing further the initial diagnosis presented in the Introduction. Three main factors were identified there that inhibit the valuing of all God's people in mission and ministry, to be addressed in turn in the three chapters of the report. Hence this chapter focuses on the second factor, the challenge of impoverishment in our understanding of the church. A richer ecclesiology is critical for the pathways to healing of our theological imagination.

The meaning of ministry

Before embarking on that task, however, it has to be acknowledged that 'ministry' is a term that can be understood in different ways by different people, and even differently by the same people in different contexts. Part of the picture is the contrasting theologies of ministry that have developed over the centuries across the spectrum of the Church of England; another is the pace of change in recent decades in the practice of ministry, with which church theology then tries to keep up. Moreover, the internal diversity and open borders of the Church of England mean that many parts of it are being influenced – and often enriched – by material on ministry produced by other churches and sometimes in other countries, notably the USA. In this situation, there is little to be gained in trying to insist on a single definition of ministry. On the other hand, proposing some common parameters for how we speak about ministry is important if we are to communicate constructively – including disagreeing in a way that may bring greater understanding – rather than simply talking past each other. That is the aim of this first section of the chapter, which offers a framework in which both the participation of all the baptized in the ministry of Christ and the designation of particular roles and responsibilities in the church as ministries can be affirmed. The next two sections then articulate in more detail how such ministries are to be understood, in relation first to theological thinking about the church and then to the specific tradition and context of the Church of England.

The lack of precision in terminology about ministry stems in part from the New Testament itself. Part of the challenge is that the earliest Christians generally used a very common, everyday word in most places where we find 'ministry' or 'minister' in English translations. *Diakonia* can also mean 'service', in the sense of what a servant does. John N. Collins, who led much of the renewed study of this area in the 1970s, looked at how the various *'diakon-'* words were used within the first-century world of the New Testament writers.[60] Collins concluded that at no point in ancient usage, Christian, pagan or secular, did they mean simply humble service to those in need. Instead, they described the service of an envoy, commissioned and accountable to perform a task. New Testament scholarship now supports this understanding of ministry as commissioned and accountable service, something done on behalf of Christ and therefore also of the church. That still leaves open the question, however, of the scope of the term, not least whether it pertains to some Christians only or to all.

One of the key biblical passages for subsequent discussion about ministry in Christian history is Ephesians 4.11–14, in which the writer talks about the gifts Christ gave once he had made captivity captive (a reference to and subversion of Psalm 68.18 in which God's victory is celebrated by the gifts he received from his captives). These gifts, that some would be apostles, prophets, evangelists, pastors and teachers, were so that everyone could 'come to the unity of the faith and of the knowledge of the Son of God, to maturity, to the measure of the full stature of Christ' (Eph. 4.13). What lies between 4.11a and 4.13 is, however, capable of being understood in two contrasting ways.

The challenge lies in where to put the commas in the English translation. Those who argue for a minimalist understanding of ministry, such as Collins, punctuate the passage like this: 'The gifts he gave were that some would be apostles, some prophets, some evangelists, some pastors and teachers, to equip the saints, for the work of ministry, for building up the body of Christ...' (Eph. 4.11–12). In other words, the gifts Christ gave achieved three things – equipping the saints, the work of ministry and the building up of the body of Christ; it was not the saints who did the work of ministry but the apostles, prophets, evangelists, pastors and teachers. Those who support a maximalist view of ministry (and indeed most modern translations), however, omit the comma between 'saints' and 'for the work of ministry.' If rendered like this, the verse makes the purpose of the gifts given to the church in apostles and others 'to equip the saints for the work of ministry', with the implied expectation that 'the work of ministry' is the task of all the saints. There are in fact good exegetical reasons for adopting this second position.[61]

On this reading, the meaning of the verse is quite straightforward: gifts were given so that that those who became apostles, prophets, evangelists, pastors and teachers could equip the saints for the work of ministry, so that everyone can 'come to the unity of the faith and of the knowledge of the Son of God, to maturity, to the measure of the full stature of Christ' (Eph. 4.13). But it is still not entirely clear whether 'the work of ministry' thus equipped by the apostles etc. is to be exercised by every individual saint, though the climax of the one long sentence in Greek that runs from verses 11 to 16 could easily be read to imply this. Its vision is of Christ as the one 'from whom the whole body, joined and knitted together by every ligament with which it is equipped, as each part is working properly, promotes the body's growth in building itself up in love' (v. 16).

The question that then needs to be considered is what 'the work of ministry' refers to in this passage, and how it relates to what we in the church today generally refer to as 'ministries' nearly two thousand years later. Is it restricted to the kind of formally authorized roles that tend to be the primary concern of 'ministry' departments at diocesan and national level, or does it encompass any kind of service offered by some to others to build up the body of Christ, or can it also refer to faithful service of Christ in the world? In considering that question, we need to keep in mind the wide range of meanings of *diakonia* and associated Greek words, encompassing both ministry and service in English. The reference to the one who wields political authority as 'God's *diakonos*' at Rom. 13.4 indicates that Paul is happy to use the language of *diakonia* in the secular sphere. While seeking to ground that language firmly in its biblical roots, we also need to shape it in a way that takes account of subsequent developments in Christian history and of the need for clear communication in our present context.

Is everyone a minister?

In light of this discussion, then, should we speak of every Christian as a minister because every Christian is commissioned for the service of Christ, or should we speak specifically of those Christians as ministers who have been formally and publicly commissioned for specific ministerial responsibilities?[62] One possible response might be to resist the implied choice here and say yes to both parts of the question. To do so, we could make a distinction between the ministry of the church, as the totality of that for which the church is commissioned by Christ, and ministries in the plural, as particular ministerial roles with associated responsibilities. All Christians share in the one ministry of the church and are ministers of Christ in that sense, with a common responsibility for using the gifts given to them for the building up of the one body. Some Christians – not all – take on particular ministerial roles that are recognized as carrying with them specific responsibilities, and are thereby ministers in this other, related and theologically secondary sense of being commissioned for one among a plurality of ministries.

That position would fit with the approach taken when discussing different kinds of vocation in the previous chapter, where a distinction was made between ministerial and social vocations. Here, ministerial vocation refers primarily to the secondary sense of 'minister' noted in the previous paragraph, to a person who receives a calling to one from among a number of particular ministries with its attendant responsibilities. This contrasts with the approach taken by the 1985 report *All Are Called*, already referred to on several occasions, where what we are here calling social vocations are designated as ministries. Although this was intended to challenge a perceived overemphasis on ordained ministry, the strategy was not ultimately very successful (as noted in the Introduction). While the meaning of ministry in Scripture and tradition is far from straightforward or one-dimensional, as has been emphasized already, it is not clear that it is quite as elastic as was being claimed. Nor does Christian service in society need to be labelled as a ministry in order to be given its proper dignity, which is rooted in humanity's calling in creation, as the first chapter emphasized.

This secondary sense of 'minister' that is intended to be invoked by the term 'ministerial vocation' as used here is defined in terms of roles that carry specific responsibilities. Such responsibilities are associated with ecclesial authority, both in terms of authorization for certain tasks and accountability to the authority of others. In the Church of England, certain kinds of authorization and accountability frame the role that is given to clergy, at ordination and also at licensing and installation to particular offices, and although there are some overlaps with lay ministries, they are partial.

The weight of the authorization and accountability placed on clergy readily attracts expectations about leadership, which has emerged as a key concern in the contemporary church. One effect of that can, evidently, be to increase the distance that may be perceived to exist not just between clergy and lay people generally but also between clergy and lay ministers, whose role is not framed in the same way. Does it, however, inevitably do this – in other words, is the distinctive nature of the responsibility historically given to ordained ministers bound to generate clericalism, as power inevitably constellates around them? How far in this context is upholding the theological distinctiveness of ordained ministries compatible with the affirmation of both equality and mutuality conveyed in Paul's description of the church as the body of Christ?

In order to take this discussion further, we need to address the question of what exactly it is that is being recognized or commissioned in different ministries. The fact that such ministries are an integral part of the life of the church leads us to explore more fully the territory of ecclesiology, mindful that the second factor identified in the initial diagnosis was an impoverishment of understanding of the church. That is the focus for the next main section.

Ministries and missional ecclesiology

The church without borders

In *Calling All God's People*, published in 2019, ecclesiological questions were treated as critical for enabling a wholehearted affirmation of the calling of the whole people of God.[63] A crucial feature of its approach was seeking to avoid – so far as possible – any assumption that 'church' is primarily a place, or a worshipping community meeting together, or an institution bearing that title, and is only secondarily the people of God seeking the kingdom of God in every part of earthly life. Hence the importance of the second paragraph of the document for the text as a whole:

> The church exists as people respond to the word and works of God, by following Christ every day in the varied circumstances of their relationships and occupations, and by meeting in Christ's name as worshiping communities, to offer praise and prayer and to receive God's grace in the ministry of word and sacrament. These two aspects of being the church should not be separated from each other, nor should one be subordinated to the other. The church is one with Christ as it shares in God's mission in every part of society, and the church is one with Christ in its joyful gathering to celebrate his resurrection.[64]

The familiar use of 'church' in English, however, to refer both to the theological reality of the body of Christ and to the building where a worshipping community regularly meets makes the association between church and place difficult to resist. It also makes it easy to imagine the church as something that can be readily marked on a map: the church is here and not there, present within these borders and absent from the geographical and social space that exists beyond them, except perhaps for occasional incursions into these habitually church-empty areas. As was argued in this report's Introduction, whatever theology of the church we might want to advocate, the various strands in secularization combine to make that look like the obvious, common-sense way to think about the church, which is why it becomes so hard to resist, especially when it comes to practical planning. Once this picture takes hold, 'church' is heard as describing primarily what happens in a place, through the institutions associated with it and via the actions and pronouncements of their publicly recognizable representatives, i.e. the clergy. Such a clericalizing ecclesiology – implicit or explicit – colludes with the secularist desire to restrict the church to a carefully boundaried zone, from which it can exercise little or no influence on 'mainstream' society.

It is a picture that can even affect attempts to counter the bias it produces, such as the language of 'gathered' and 'sent' church used in *Setting God's People Free*.[65] Where are we gathered to, and where are we sent from? The risk is that the strength of association between church and place makes it easy to hear such language as making a distinction between being gathered *into* the church and being sent out *from* the church – with the clear implication that it is in gathering that the church is most truly at home and most truly itself: the gathered church sits at the centre, with the sent church always moving away from that centre. Keeping in mind the primacy of God's agency in gathering and sending can help to counter this: the church as gathered by and in God is not defined by geographical or social boundaries, while the church as sent by God always travels in divine company and never moves away from its divine origin. If we can resist the centripetal force that wants to locate the church in this place rather than that place, so that it is only really at home in the world here and not there, then the dynamic of gathering and sending can be described in ways that do not constantly insert a boundary between where the church is and where the church is not. For example, we are free to think of the church gathering the world into the praise of God through the presence within the world of redeemed humanity, or of the church's members being sent from the world into the assembly of the church to intercede for those parts of their community and society bound up with their social and relational vocations.

At the same time, *Calling All God's People* also sought to resist the understandable corrective response that the church is primarily found in the daily lives of Christian disciples, or in activities that seek the coming of God's kingdom in various spheres of society. In an age that is suspicious of institutions and in which it is expected that the deepest meaning of our lives is independent from them, attempts to disconnect the meaning of church from institutional forms – which have antecedents in eighteenth- and nineteenth-century thought – have an enduring but ultimately self-destructive attraction.[66] For the reaction to the impoverishment of the understanding of the church that reduces it to a social institution with centres that may be marked on a map cannot be to imagine that social institutions are irrelevant to it.

The human calling is to live in historical time as social creatures, who build and sustain institutions in order to give some permanence to forms of shared meaning and participation in common goods, common objects of love. As emphasized in the previous chapter, this belongs to our created humanity, and the church is humanity redeemed in all its creaturely richness, not thinned out to be disembodied spirits. That richness encompasses the fundamental role of ritual for social existence, together with the accumulating tapestry of commentary and the symbolic actions associated with it. Anglican tradition includes the description of the church as a 'visible society', and as such it is a society configured in profound ways by its festal gathering week by week on the Lord's day to share in word and sacrament. There is therefore something properly precious about the gathering together of God's people for praise and prayer every Sunday and on the great festivals of the church, and it is to be expected that the buildings that are used for that purpose over years, decades and centuries in specific places should hold a particular value for us. Many creative forms of participation in church life were evident during the recent period when public worship in church buildings was not permitted in this country, yet something was also palpably lost when church buildings were locked and Christians could not share face to face in worship, including the sacraments.

Who we are in God's mission

The present report aims to continue the approach taken in *Calling All God's People* by sustaining an understanding of the church as always both people commissioned together for service in the world by their union with Christ and people dwelling in deepening communion with one another by their union with Christ. Neither can be made prior to the other; both are integral to what it means to be 'in Christ' and there is always a dynamic interrelationship between them, a fundamental rhythm that extends to every area of Christian life. Nothing that we do in Christ is either solely about presence and service in the world for which Christ died, or solely about communion with others who trust in him; it is always about both together. We cannot belong to Christ without participating in his mission, and we cannot belong to Christ without being members one of another. This is not a new insight but an affirmation that has been repeated across the churches numerous times over the past century:

> We who have been chosen in Christ, reconciled to God through Him, made members of His Body, sharers in His Spirit, and heirs through hope of His Kingdom, are by these very facts committed to full participation in His redeeming mission. There is no participation in Christ without participation in His mission to the world.[67]

This report also seeks to build on these insights and develop them. As mentioned in the Introduction, the Faith and Order Commission has been working towards a document on missional ecclesiology, which would provide one way to frame an answer to the question: what can we say the church is, in every context where it is present? That question might also be re-phrased as: what do we say we are, in every context where we are present? Ecclesiology is about the church's self-understanding, which means, if we believe ourselves to belong to the church, that it concerns our own self-understanding. As such, ecclesiology is pivotal for shaping our theological imagination: it is about who we think we are, all the time and in every situation – unless, once again, our minds have been colonized by an individualism that tells us that who we truly are is ultimately detached from our union with one another in Christ, and that the church is simply a human organization or community that we visit from time to time.

Missional ecclesiology begins with the insight that 'who we are' as the church is a community called by Christ for the sake of the world, in line with the emphasis in the previous chapter on vocation in Christ always being given for and with others. One of the pioneers of missional ecclesiology in the contemporary context was Lesslie Newbigin, according to whom 'The church lives in the midst of history as sign, instrument, and foretaste of the reign of God,' a formulation taken up in some significant ecumenical texts.[68] That is one way to describe who we are, as the church, all the time, in every part of our lives. We are the sign, instrument and foretaste of the kingdom as we fulfil different roles within society, and as two or three meet together in Christ's name in a family or household, and as we gather for the liturgical assembly week by week. We are the church in each of these contexts: we are not 'more' the church in one of them than the other, and we can only truly be the church in any of them if we are open to being the church in all of them.

Crucially, that means that ministerial vocations, as defined in the present report, are not more 'central' to the church than social vocations or relational vocations. Indeed, social and relational vocations have an essential role in providing ways of living out our self-understanding as the church of God consistently. Accepting a specific form of life-shaping commitment relating to work or to relationships as a response to God's call is a way of affirming that in that work and in that relationship I am truly part of the church, sharing in the mission that defines the church, taking my part in being the sign, instrument and foretaste of God's new society, the city of God. Recent experiences of the suspension of public worship together in one place because of the Covid-19 pandemic have helped many to come to a renewed appreciation of the relationship between the church as festal assembly, the church in home and family,[69] and the church in everyday discipleship. The first or the second of those may be denied us, for a short time or indefinitely, and, as already stated, without them something is lost. Even without them, though, we are still the church, still called to be sign, instrument and foretaste of God's kingdom in our sharing together in the mission of Christ that reaches into all the world. If we are not willing to share in that mission, we distance ourselves from the reality of the church, as surely as if we cease to care about meeting together for public worship.

Beginning with baptism

To say that these different contexts are all part of the life of the church in the mission of God is not to say that they are all the same. The liturgical assembly for word and sacrament teaches and makes visible to us who we are in a unique way. The Eucharist, for instance, is the sacrament of our baptismal union with Christ and the unity the baptized thereby have with one another. In it, the whole of our lives is gathered up in the church's offering of praise and thanksgiving, and our identity is affirmed as the body of Christ in which the world is transformed, that its fractured kingdoms may become the kingdom of God. The church that assembles to celebrate the eucharist is the one church that walks together through the world on the manifold paths of discipleship. In the eucharistic assembly, there is an unparalleled transparency of the church as sign, instrument and foretaste of the kingdom of God.

In baptism, we come with our varied relationships, commitments and responsibilities to be united to Christ in his death and resurrection, and to be commissioned to live as his disciples every day of our lives, in the midst of those relationships, commitments and responsibilities. The baptismal liturgy in the Church of England powerfully expresses the call of the people of God in Christ to service in the world and to communion with one another as two parts of a dynamic whole: baptism is both entry into that communion, which includes sharing in the Eucharist, and commissioning for Christ's service in every part of our lives. The Common Worship baptism service includes a section headed the 'Commission', in which the pattern of life that follows from being united with Christ in baptism is set out. It begins by stating: 'Those who are baptized are called to worship and serve God.' All who have been baptized share together in this calling, united as one royal priesthood. As such, all Christians share in the calling of the church to represent Christ and make him known in the world. The minister says to each candidate in the Church of England's baptism service: 'Shine as a light in the world to the glory of God the Father.'

One of the themes in liturgical renewal over the past century has been that baptism is not something that happened to us some time ago, but a present reality, a mystery into whose depths there is always further to go. The location of baptism at the heart of the Easter Liturgy, the centre of gravity for the church's year, can be a powerful expression of that truth.[70] A number of these themes are brought together in words with which the bishop introduces the Common Worship ordination service:

> God calls his people to follow Christ, and forms us into a royal priesthood, a holy nation, to declare the wonderful deeds of him who has called us out of darkness into his marvellous light.
>
> The Church is the Body of Christ, the people of God and the dwelling-place of the Holy Spirit. In baptism the whole Church is summoned to witness to God's love and to work for the coming of his kingdom.[71]

There is a rich theology here of ministry as the calling of the whole church. There may be value in reflecting on how ordination services can be conducted in such a way that both the 'choreography' of the liturgy and the commentary on it offered at key points affirms and opens up that theology for all who are present. The same could be said also of induction and licensing services.

The church as a whole has been commissioned by God for service, 'to declare the wonderful deeds of him who has called us out of darkness into his marvellous light', by actions and words together. The church has a ministry, then, and all the baptized have a share in this ministry and indeed a responsibility for this ministry. As stated in a text from the International Anglican Liturgical Consultation, 'Baptism affirms the royal dignity of every Christian and their call and empowering for active ministry within the mission of the church.... A true understanding of baptism will bring with it a new expectancy about the ministry of each Christian.'[72] This theme is developed powerfully in the latest document from the Anglican – Roman Catholic International Commission, *Walking Together on the Way*:

> All the baptized are initiated into the *tria munera Christi,* that is, the threefold office and mission of Christ as *prophet, priest,* and *king,* and each is called to an active sharing in that ministry. Each of the baptized shares in Christ's role as *prophet*, because baptism makes one receptive to the Word of God, and the Spirit of truth impels the baptized to share the Good News (Rom 8:14–15). Similarly, each shares in the ministry of Christ as priest inasmuch as each participates in Christ's own salvific death and his resurrection (see Rom 6.5–11). Bound to each other in Christ, each of the baptized, guided by the Spirit, likewise exercises a priestly ministry by acting

as Christ's instrument for the salvation of others. The baptized also share in Christ's role as *king*. Subject to Christ's kingship, they are directed to the fullness of his kingdom as their eschatological goal. The loving adoption that is received in baptism urges the faithful to have care for the eternal and present welfare of everyone they encounter (2 Cor 5.14ff). Thus, the baptismal vocation of all those reborn in water and the Spirit demands that they exercise the *tria munera Christi*; that they expect to be ministered to by other Christians who also participate in the threefold office of Christ; and that they give thanks for the gifts deriving from nothing else than the infinitely loving initiative of God. But this participation is no individualistic or purely local matter, for Christians do not belong to Christ without having a relationship with others who likewise belong to Christ because the Spirit has given to each a birth to new life in Christ (see TCTCV §41).[73]

Diversity without hierarchy

As was affirmed in the previous section of this chapter, then, every Christian shares in the ministry of Christ that has been entrusted to the church and, as such, every Christian is a minister. At the same time, some Christians are commissioned for ministries that are recognized roles in the church with specific responsibilities, and they may also be called ministers in this secondary sense. We have just been commenting on the significance of the liturgical assembly for articulating the mystery of the church's being. It should not therefore be surprising that the responsibilities associated with some ministries include liturgical tasks: presiding, preaching, blessing, absolving, baptizing. Similarly, these liturgical tasks may both reflect and express responsibilities that some ministers carry for the whole of the church's life, such as proclaiming the gospel, making disciples and feeding Christ's flock. This liturgical dimension of ministries is pivotal for the understanding of ordained ministry in the Church of England:

> Exercising leadership in worship is central to the ordained minister's formational role in building up the body. Worship is also the source

and resource for the ordained minister's leadership in mission, exercising a public and representative role for the church and expressing God's work of transformation in the world.[74]

Yet there is always a danger that the liturgical assembly comes to appear as more truly or fully the church than the church serving Christ day by day in homes, communities and institutions. As long as we remember that the church we are when gathering for word and sacrament is the same church we are in everyday discipleship, and that we cannot say yes to being the church in the weekly assembly without saying yes to being the church in our daily sharing in Christ's mission, then the danger is limited. Once we let our thinking be shaped by a deficient ecclesiology, however, one that colludes with the exclusion of the church from public space in a secularized society, then the Sunday meeting comes increasingly to fill the entire horizon of what church means. Along with this, those who hold specific roles within that meeting for worship begin to loom large as those who control the church, perhaps even as those who produce the church for consumption by others and have exclusive responsibility for it. Moreover, the necessary boundaries between the tasks in the Sunday liturgy that are reserved to ordained ministers, those that may be taken on by licensed or authorized ministries, and those that are common to all then begin to acquire the character of a hierarchy; the most restricted tasks are deemed the most privileged and therefore the most important, with corresponding prestige attaching to those who exercise them, potentially triggering destructive cycles of envy and pride.

We need a thoroughly missional ecclesiology in order to value diverse ministries in their distinctiveness, grounded in the truth that the church is first and foremost all who share together in the service of God's kingdom, and not a pattern of activity controlled by others to which we happen to affiliate ourselves. Such an ecclesiology can help to renew our theological imagination about what the church is and where it is to be found. Which vision of the church does our church website, for instance, convey – what stories does it tell to express what the life of the church consists in and how this can be encountered?

How then should it be decided which roles, with what responsibilities, should be designated as belonging among the formally recognized ministries which contribute to the one ministry of the whole church, given so that we may grow together into the fullness of Christ? The focus for the final section of this chapter will be on the Church of England, but it may be helpful to think in general terms of actions authorized by the church by which the church seeks 'to declare the wonderful deeds of him who has called us out of darkness into his marvellous light'. Worship, sacraments, preaching and teaching, pastoral care, evangelism, social outreach – all would be encompassed within that, together with the varied activities that support them, from administration and governance to the maintenance of buildings and care of the material things that are required. It is perfectly possible to contribute to such ministries without having a specific vocation in the sense outlined in the previous chapter of a life-shaping commitment to them. We do not need to have a vocation as a church cleaner to be on the rota for this: we can just see that there is good work to be done, and that it is good for us to do it. Indeed, it is essential that there be a strong sense of shared responsibility for the common ministry of the church and of shared participation in it, with particular ministries being no more and no less than recognized ways of responding to that. To return to an example discussed in the Introduction, the twentieth-century Liturgical Movement sought to recover an awareness that the whole congregation acts together in the church's worship and celebrates the sacraments together, and that there is no ministry greater or more important than this, which is shared by all. Some, properly and necessarily, are in addition called to officiate and preside, but such a particular ministerial vocation is only given to serve the whole people of God in fulfilling their common and glorious calling.

Interdependence of ministries

In this section of the chapter, we return to the second of the two clusters of questions flagged at the start: how is the relationship to be conceived between ordained and other forms of ministry, and is it possible to avoid presenting the latter as essentially subordinate to the former? The argument of the chapter so far has been that all particular ministries need to be understood as serving the one common ministry of the whole church. That may be contested as a point of departure: there are versions of both Protestant and Catholic ecclesiology in which it is the apostolic ministry of some that creates and sustains the apostolic church. That would seem to depend, however, on isolating the apostolic ministry as something other than the action of the church. If we accept that there is no church without ministry, and no ministry without church, then a debate about which comes first is misguided, as is one about the historical primacy of the ministry of the whole church as against the ministry of word and sacrament exercised by some. Again, the two are inseparable: neither can be 'derived' from the other, as each depends on the other.[75]

'From the Apostles' time'

Nonetheless, the Church of England teaches that some ministries are apostolic in a way that others are not: according to the Preface to the sixteenth-century Ordinal, 'It is evident unto all men diligently reading holy Scripture and ancient Authors, that from the Apostles' time there have been these Orders of Ministers in Christ's Church; Bishops, Priests, and Deacons.'[76] That is not to say, however, that these are the only ministries that the church needs, but it is to assert that they are the ministries needed in every age, while others that are required to complement them may change over time. Moreover, within these three, the order of bishops has a specific responsibility for maintaining apostolic continuity, in teaching, in mission and in the ordaining others to them. As such, the ministry of the bishop includes oversight of all other ministries in the life of the church, both lay and ordained. As 'Ministry for a Christian Presence' (2019) expresses it,

> bishops bear the responsibility collectively and individually for the consistency and authenticity of all ministries exercised in the name of the Church, and thus directly, or through others, for the discernment, formation and sustenance of all ministers.[77]

The ministry of bishops, priests and deacons emerges in a form recognizable from the standpoint of later centuries in documents dating from the second and third centuries. In this early period, what the ordained ministries of deacon, priest and bishop provided was continuity over time for the church in each place and, through the ministry of the bishops specifically, connection with the church in other places, through the exchange of letters and visits and through periodic gatherings of church councils. Other forms of publicly recognized ministry are also clearly visible alongside them: prophets and teachers, as well as apostles at the start of the period. Indeed, some of the most influential figures from this time were not ordained as deacons, bishops or priests, such as the teacher and philosopher Justin Martyr. Origen, the most significant writer from the second and third centuries in terms of subsequent influence on theology and spirituality, was only ordained after he had been a prominent teacher with a public position in the church for many years, and even then in somewhat ambiguous and contested circumstances. Leadership in the church was also exercised by those who had suffered for their faith in persecutions, some of whom were ordained while some were not. In the fourth and fifth centuries such leaders included monks living an ascetic life, who at that point were normally not ordained, monasticism being originally a lay movement in the life of the church. Although in the course of the Middle Ages the vision of monasticism as primarily a movement of lay discipleship was largely lost, religious communities and individuals living under religious vows continued to provide something of a counterpoint to the ministry offered by diocesan clergy.

Nonetheless, there was also from the beginning a tendency for ordained ministry to absorb other, originally distinct forms of ministry. The gradual domination during the Middle Ages of male religious communities by members ordained to the priesthood would be one example. Already in the second century, the ministry of those still calling themselves 'apostles' as they exercised an itinerant ministry was being displaced by the apostolic ministry of bishops. From the fourth century onwards, those recognized as teachers of the faith were likely to be ordained as bishops, priests or deacons, while in the later part of the Middle Ages in Western Europe, any public ministry on the part of those not ordained, including female members of religious communities, tended to be closely supervised and monitored by those who were.

The Church of England following the Reformation

When the Church of England emerged from the upheavals of the mid-sixteenth century, it had lost the religious communities of monks, nuns and friars as an alternative locus for Christian ministry, and also abolished the 'minor orders' of lector (reader), acolytes, exorcists, doorkeepers and cantors. These had provided liturgical roles with associated responsibilities for people other than bishops, priests and deacons, but they were not directly replaced. Although various forms of assistance came to be provided, as will be discussed further below, and the picture has changed significantly in more recent times, the Church of England norm for public worship in this period became liturgy under the sole direction of the parish priest, his voice alone in dialogue with the congregation. Moreover, the effect of the seventeenth-century upheavals was to discourage the cultivation of the home as a place of gathering for daily prayer, praise and study of the Scriptures, because of its association with those whom their adversaries dubbed 'Puritans', rendered suspect as a church context beyond the immediate supervision of the clergy.

While some reformed churches dispensed with deacons and bishops, in the Church of England the three major orders inherited from medieval Christendom were retained and, in the course of the seventeenth century, vigorously defended as deriving from the dispensation of the apostles.[78] With diaconal ministry now normally only a brief prelude to priesthood, the Church of England was left with a relatively narrow range of publicly recognized offices holding ministerial authority in the church's life. It might look, from one perspective, rather more clerical and indeed more male than it had in the late Middle Ages, when Julian of Norwich and Margery Kempe could still exercise their rather different ministries.

On the other hand, in the realm of church governance, lay people were exercising authority in significantly new ways in England in the sixteenth and seventeenth centuries, beginning with the monarch as Supreme Governor of the Church of England and Parliament as the body that approved ecclesiastical legislation. As new Anglican Churches began to be established through missionary endeavour in other countries from the later eighteenth century onwards, they set up Synods and Councils in which lay people shared with bishops and clergy in the responsibilities of governance. That model was then brought back to the Church of England after the First World War with the introduction of the Church Assembly as a national body with lay representation, and of Parochial Church Councils with elected members. Nor should the parish priest be thought of as existing before that in isolation: provision for the appointment of Churchwardens was made in the canons of 1604, while the priest would also expect there to be a parish clerk, usually a layman, to assist in the care of the building and lead the people in the responses during public worship, sometimes also reading one of the lessons. Yet despite the significant responsibilities and indeed authority held by those occupying these various offices, the title of 'Minister' was generally restricted in the Church of England to those ordained to the ministry of word and sacrament as deacons, priests and bishops.

Some blurring of the lines occurred early in the reign of Elizabeth I. Clergy numbers were in decline and many parish churches were without ministry of word or sacrament. The office of Reader, previously abolished with the other minor orders of the medieval church, was revived in 1559, and the Act of Uniformity published that year refers in several places to 'Parson, vicar, or other whatsoever minister'. Archbishop Parker responded to the crisis in the church with some hasty ordinations, including at first the ordination of Lectors (Readers), though after that year Readers were commissioned, appointed or admitted by licence or 'toleration' of their Ordinary (bishop), not ordained. During the first two years of Elizabeth's reign, Parker appointed more than seventy Readers, and it is clear that most were running parishes alone, though they were forbidden to preach, or to minister the sacraments, and once an incumbent arrived in the parish their services were no longer required. Over time, clergy numbers increased, but Readers continued to minister in English parishes until well into the eighteenth century.

Another crisis led to the re-introduction of the office of Reader in 1866. It followed the realization, after the 1851 census, that the vast majority of the urban poor were unchurched. The task of these new Readers was to be an authorized and qualified 'bridge' between the established and clerically led church and the un-churched and often anti-church population. Readers were appointed to be teachers, catechists and evangelists. The nineteenth century also saw new initiatives that gave fresh scope to what we would now recognize as lay ministry within the Church of England, including the revival of religious communities of women, often focused on pastoral ministry of various kinds. In 1882, the Church Army was founded by Wilson Carlisle as a voluntary association of lay evangelists that provided an Anglican alternative to the work of the Salvation Army. The order of deaconesses came into existence in 1861 and by the end of the century there were also other forms of women's ministry recognized by the Church of England, including female missioners and Church Army sisters.

This renewed diversity of ministries continued to flourish in the later part of the twentieth century. The changing context created by ordination of women was accompanied by the revival of the permanent (or distinctive) diaconate in the Church of England – initially through it being opened to women while priesthood and the episcopate remained closed, but then becoming a valued form of ministerial vocation for women and men alike. While numbers remain relatively low, it is nonetheless a matter of some significance that there now are people who find the heart of their vocation in each of the three historic orders of ministry, not just in Anglican churches but in other global communions as well.[79]

The variety of ministries today

Lay ministry has continued to grow and develop in new ways. As 'Ministry for a Christian Presence' comments, 'The range of lay ministries is constantly developing in response to God's gift and call.'[80] Both lay and ordained pioneer ministers are leading fresh expressions and planting churches; many dioceses have commissioned pastoral workers/assistants, evangelists and children, youth or family workers – and the list could easily be continued. As this very brief review suggests, it is important to register that changes in lay ministries have been interwoven with changes in ordained ministries, and indeed in the relationship between them. Interdependence between ordained and other ministries, however flawed, undervalued and threatened it may have been by ignorance and sin, has always been a reality. All belong together in serving the one ministry of the one church and in contributing to its common good; none can stand in isolation. In order to be the sign, instrument and foretaste of the kingdom in this age, the church needs all the gifts that Christ has given to its members, expressed in the diversity of its many ministries woven together under the direction of the Holy Spirit.

Generalization is hazardous, especially given the relative freedom dioceses possess to develop lay ministry in a way that fits their vision, priorities and needs. There is, however, a renewed awareness today of the importance of flexibility and creativity in authorizing and simply encouraging many other ministries in the Church of England alongside ordained ministries. These too are needed 'for building up the body of Christ'. The remarkable proliferation of names and types of lay ministry that is happening was noted in the Introduction. Some of them will be roles that people take on for a limited period, some roles that, as with ordained ministries, they take on for life – that become a lasting vocation. Some will be associated with well-established patterns of ministry, while others may be invited to explore new paths and speak with a radical and prophetic challenge. Some will be supported by resources from the institutional church, including financial contribution, while most will be self-supporting, with such ministries held in many cases alongside social vocations to other kinds of work and social context, as is often the case too for self-supporting clergy.

Of course, there are all kinds of overlap between ordained and lay ministries, but interdependence implies distinction as well as relationship. Within the work of ministry in the Church of England, clergy are called both to specific responsibilities and to a pattern of life. This picture is set out in its historic formularies, its contemporary ordination services and its ecclesiastical legislation. As already noted, the Church of England holds that the three orders of ministry – deacon, priest and bishop – have been given to the whole church of God in the providence of God and derive from the ministry of the apostles. That does not mean that all the roles and tasks associated with these orders stay the same forever; indeed, we are living through a time of significant transition in this respect.

Nonetheless, there remains a recognizable affinity in very broad terms between the position of the contemporary Church of England and the thumbnail sketch of the second and third centuries given earlier in this section of the chapter. The ministry of bishops and those ordained by them has a unique role in sustaining within the universal church the continuity of the local church over time and the connection of the local church across space. Anglican ecclesiology since the Reformation has generally allowed that it is possible in exceptional circumstances for the church to survive without such ministry but does not envisage it ever becoming dispensable in the life of the universal church.[81] The ministry of bishops and those ordained by them therefore establishes certain parameters for all ministry, not least in the responsibility of oversight for the whole life of the diocese that is given to bishops and expressed in their appointment of parish clergy to share with them in the 'cure of souls' in that place. That oversight, however, is to foster the growth of all the varied ministries that are needed alongside ordained ministries if the church of God is to flourish. 'From the apostles' time' there have been ordained ministries and all kinds of other ministries alongside them, serving together the one ministry of the whole church. Ordained ministries have a fixity that sustains the continuity of the church over time. Other ministries have a fluidity that is essential as the church responds to the ever-changing challenges of mission.

In the contemporary context, the Church of England finds itself at a particular moment in the response to the dynamics of secularization that were mentioned in the Introduction and discussed further in the previous chapter. Renewal and Reform, as a national initiative launched by the Archbishops in 2015, marks a determination – criticized by some – to focus resources on fostering missional activity that can serve the growth of the church as new people are drawn into the paths of discipleship. An integral part of this has been an emphasis on the importance of leadership at every level of church life in enabling both creative thinking about missional activity and strategic planning that enables appropriate prioritization to take effect. This has sparked important debate about the relationship between leadership and ministry, and indeed about the form of leadership that is needed in the life of the church.[82] One model of leadership within our culture is to allow power and authority to become concentrated, following due selection and training, in the hands of someone who, with careful accountability in terms of governance, is given maximum scope in terms of running the organization to implement the changes they think necessary. That model, if uncritically transferred to the church context, is both bound to distort the interdependence of ministries that has been the theme of this section and also likely to mesh happily with persistent strains of clericalism. Other models would advocate the value of growing leadership of different kinds across the life of an institution, with oversight of unfolding initiatives and the health of the whole as the critical responsibility for those who have greater degrees of authority. Such models are more congruent with what is being advocated here.

It should therefore be expected that a variety of recognized and commissioned lay ministries will be needed alongside ordained ministries in order for the church in each place to respond to God's call to share in God's mission, and that this variety will not be the same in each case. The priority needs to be that there is an effective response to that call that brings together the gifts God has given to the whole people of God, for the sake of the whole work of God, as is brought out by Paul in 1 Cor. 12.12–31 with its link at the end to the celebration of self-giving love in 1 Cor. 13. No one is given a ministry for their own benefit or so that they can exercise control over others. The more authority that is given to a person in ministry, the greater the responsibility to elicit the gifts of all God's people and enable the full panoply of ministries needed for the church to be fruitful in God's mission.

Rivalry for status and resources, misuse of power made easier by the imbalance of power, territorial behaviour that cannot bear to relinquish an inch of control: these things are, of course, no more absent from the Church in the twenty-first century than they were in the first, the third or the sixteenth. Naivety about this or deliberate looking away from the reality of human sinfulness will not help the healing of theological vision that is needed if ours is to be the generation that overcomes the long-standing frustrations within the Church of England about the ministry of the whole people of God. Despite this, the church still has the opportunity to live in a radically different kind of way, eschewing worldly arguments for the sake of Christian mutuality – seeking to build each other up and bear each other's burdens, and finding ways to live together with mutual trust and appreciation for the different gifts that each brings. It has been said by many people – so many, in fact, that it is hard to trace the original source for the quotation – that the Church of God does not so much have a mission as the mission of God has a church. The mission is so important and the need so great that we must draw on the gifts of all God's people for it, and there is a price to pay for neglecting or slighting the contribution of any. There is to be no place for competition or contest here, but rather rejoicing in the abundance of the giver.

Challenges for ministry

This chapter has argued that fostering an understanding of ministries that sets them in right relationship to one another and to the life of the church is vital for healing our theological vision of the church as sign, instrument and foretaste of God's kingdom.

To do that, we face significant challenges.

- 'Minister' can be used as a title that sets some Christians apart from others. We should be clear both that every Christian is called in baptism to share in the one ministry of Christ and therefore to minister in the name of Christ, and that Christ also calls some people to forms of service in the church that are recognized by the church as particular ministries. That means taking care with our language.

- Particular ministries come with distinctive responsibilities, including those associated with authority and leadership. They can tempt those entrusted with them to a love of status and power. For others, they can become a focus for envy and resentment. Appreciating the gifts of the Holy Spirit amongst us makes spiritual demands upon us. We need to watch what is going on in our hearts as well as what we say in public.

- As sign, instrument and foretaste of God's kingdom, the church cannot be located in a place on a map or confined in religious institutions. The church is those who in union with Christ share in the mission of Christ and have communion with one another. Ministerial vocations are not therefore more 'central' to the life of the church than social or relational vocations. We will not be able to get them in proper perspective unless we grasp this.

- Ministries are among the gifts of the Holy Spirit to the church to enable it to share in Christ's mission in the world. There are three orders of ministry that give continuity and connection to the pattern of the church's life: bishops, priests and deacons. They exist alongside and in relation to the many other ministries given by God whose changing forms respond to the changing circumstances of mission. Pressure on resources in a post-Christendom context makes it tempting to view such ministries primarily as a means to fill gaps left by reductions in ordained ministries. If we are to value the gifts God is giving us, we have to resist this.

Chapter3 Discipleship: Looking to Jesus

Discipleship and the kingdom of God

Christians are people who have heard the call of the God of creation through Jesus Christ. As was mentioned in the first chapter, the stories in the Gospels of those who responded to meeting Jesus by following him and becoming his disciples have served as a rich resource throughout Christian history for reflecting on what it means in the present moment to say 'yes' to Christ. They show both the variety of vocations that may be received because of that 'yes', and their unity as interweaving paths for following the same Lord of all creation towards a common home in the new heaven and the new earth.

This final chapter on discipleship, then, is intended to explore that unity in discipleship further and address some of the shared challenges for us in our varied vocations and ministries, notably in the second section, 'Formation on the Frontline'. With regard to the preceding chapter, the relationship between ecclesiology and discipleship is a focus in this first section, while the third section proposes discipleship as the guiding horizon as well as common ground for all particular ministries. Part of the aim of the chapter, therefore, is to use the theme of discipleship to draw together some of the main threads from the report so far.

As was suggested in the Introduction, however, discipleship has specific challenges in the disorientating context of a post-Christendom society. Much around us can look familiar and friendly to faith, yet there are plenty of voices warning us that we are in a hostile environment. Then again, others inside and outside the church will insist that a secular culture is one that is essentially neutral in religious matters, and that to ask whether its features and dynamics are for or against the gospel is to miss the point. The root of the disease we have been trying to combat throughout this report recurs here as a persistent and powerful temptation: acceptance that faith in Christ relates to a limited zone within our experience, defined by community activities, institutional life and individual devotions, so that we both give up on the unity of all things in Christ and invest the small world we mistake for the church with distorting expectations. The pathway to healing must include the doctrine of creation and the doctrine of the church, as explored in the previous chapters, but all in relation to Christology with its central question: 'Who do you say I am?' (Mark 8.29).

Discipleship at the centre?

Discipleship as a subject for Christian theology has become hard to detach from the lectures by Dietrich Bonhoeffer from the mid-1930s in Germany that were eventually published as *Discipleship* – the simple title Bonhoeffer gave his book, though rendered as *The Cost of Discipleship* in the first English translation. Bonhoeffer was alert to the apparent disappearance of discipleship language in the Pauline letters but argued that the stress on faith found there could not be separated from the teaching on discipleship in the Gospels, as if somehow Paul had arrived at a higher understanding than Jesus of Nazareth. Baptism for him was a vital thread connecting the two, as both act of faith in Christ and entry into the way of discipleship.[83] We have already had occasion to comment on the significance of baptism in relation to vocation and to ministry in the previous two chapters, and Bonhoeffer's insight on this point confirms its importance for the theme of this one as well.

Bonhoeffer's immediate concern in his lectures was that the neglect of discipleship for a self-consciously 'Pauline' faith was fostering a complacent mentality among those accustomed to the benefits of Christendom at the very point where Christianity itself was being threatened by a mortal enemy. Discipleship means commitment, costly commitment, not just receiving a gift that changes nothing; it means life in community with other disciples, not just an individual relationship with Jesus; it means seeking and striving to grow in faithfulness, not just waiting for God to do something; and it means taking up the cross every day, and facing the evil of death, not holding on to every place of apparent security and safety while the flood is creeping up on us. We live in times that are very different from Bonhoeffer's, yet his urgent pleading for the rediscovery of the power of following Jesus in the face of a socially acceptable Christianity that fosters indifference to his call continues to resonate powerfully with many today.

Discipleship has not been without its critics, however, as a way of framing Christian life in late-modern, post-Christendom society. The association of discipleship with a choice to follow Christ that knows the cost of leaving behind the ways of the world may appeal to some. On the other hand, it might be countered that to frame Christianity in this way pushes away people for whom there might still be some resonance with Christian faith but who would not (for various reasons) see the natural expression of this in membership of a community committed to a distinctive form of life characterized by social contrast. Arguing that discipleship is a 'theologically peripheral concept', Linda Woodhead proposed we should be concentrating instead on developing a 'societal' understanding of church that would renew a more extended sense of Christian identity.[84] There are a number of strands to Woodhead's argument, including how to judge the effects of secularization and the emergence of a social situation characterized in this report as 'post-Christendom'. For our purposes, the crucial issue is whether, if it is true that 'societal Churches go out into society; congregational ones try to bring society into church', as Woodhead writes, then a focus on discipleship is bound to weigh ecclesiology in a 'congregational' direction. Support for that claim might be sought in Loveday Alexander's contrast 'between two different ecclesiologies: an ecclesiology of discipleship (messianic community) and an ecclesiology of the Kingdom (renewal of the whole people of God)'. Alexander traces these two ecclesiologies through the Gospels and argues that they are often in tension with each other, with 'discipleship as following' leading naturally to a more intentional, inward focused and bounded church, a contrast society.[85]

When she made these remarks, Woodhead was reacting against a renewed emphasis on discipleship in documents associated with the launch of the Archbishops' Renewal and Reform initiative in 2015, including a report on 'Developing Discipleship' that was debated at the General Synod.[86] Woodhead agreed with the Archbishops that the continual and accelerating decline of Christian belief and affiliation is not in fact inevitable, though she proposed a very different kind of response. If it is true that an emphasis on discipleship tends to set the church against the world, placing borders around it that serve to reduce its presence in the eyes of those both inside and outside them, then that emphasis would hardly seem to be the best starting point for addressing the problems identified in this report of weak theological imagination in how Christians see their involvement in society, limited understanding of the mystery of the church, and perplexity in the face of powerful cultural currents about worth, work and fulfilment. These are, the Introduction argued, three critical factors that undermine the Church of England's affirmation of the calling of all God's people.

It becomes apparent in Bonhoeffer's exposition, however, that discipleship is not a one-dimensional concept in the way that line of critique seems to suggest, not least because of its anchorage in such diverse narratives and sayings in the Gospels. To be a disciple is, literally, to be a learner, but to learn from Christ is not primarily a matter of academic study or intellectual knowledge. It involves being transformed by his constant company in everyday life so that we may fulfil the various tasks he lays upon us and may do as he would have us do. According to Mark's Gospel, 'And he appointed twelve, whom he also named apostles, to be with him, and to be sent out to proclaim the message, and to have authority to cast out demons' (Mark 3.14–15). Not all disciples are apostles, but that dynamic relationship between staying close to Christ to attend to him ('to be with him') and being sent out by Christ to share in his works characterizes all discipleship. Whatever we may do in his name must flow from being with him. It is also true that we cannot draw near to be with him without being called by him to go and act for him, making disciples of all nations in obedience to him.

There is an affinity here with the dynamic movement within ecclesiology that was emphasized in the previous chapter between deepening communion and sharing in mission, both being generated from the church's union in Christ. The variety of prepositions we can draw from the Gospels is relevant here: those who believe in Christ and follow him must dwell with him and indeed in him, as he in them (in the language of John), but they must also follow 'after him' as the one who goes ahead of them and perform tasks he sends them out to do in his name. The disciple who is sent out by Jesus to a new place, or back to a familiar place, goes as his follower and is therefore always travelling towards him, not away from him. It is that transforming journey of following Jesus as his disciples that is explored in the current chapter.

Christ in our midst

In this light, discipleship and kingdom are not so much contrasting as complementary themes, especially when seen in light of Christology. Jesus taught his followers to 'strive first for the kingdom of God and his righteousness' (Matt. 6.33): seeking the kingdom is what disciples do, but always with their eyes on the one whom they follow. The New Testament makes it clear that God's kingly rule is uniquely present in the person of Jesus Christ, and that following him therefore draws us into the kingdom and begins to unravel sin's disruption of creation, as we pray in his name, 'your kingdom come; your will be done on earth as in heaven'. Origen, a theologian of the early church, explained that Jesus is 'the kingdom in person' (*autobasileia*). As disciples of the Son of God, in following him we are therefore seeking God's kingdom in and through him, and in striving for the kingdom we are branches of the one vine, able to bear fruit insofar as we remain in him, enlivened by union with him. The coming of God's kingdom on earth can only mean the glorification of God's Son, just as the acknowledgment of Jesus of Nazareth as Lord must finally come from all creation. Our halting steps in discipleship are inseparable from the hope expressed in the vision of Revelation: 'The kingdom of the world has become the kingdom of our Lord and of his Messiah, and he will reign for ever and ever' (Rev. 11.15).

The meaning of discipleship hinges on the identity of the one to whom we are attending and are committed to following; to see oneself as a disciple means facing and answering the pivotal question of the Synoptic Gospels – 'But who do you say that I am?' (Mark 8.29). It is Christology, then, that both defines and gives depth to discipleship. A Christology that confines the presence of Christ in the world to the gathering of believers for word and sacrament is indeed likely to generate an understanding of discipleship that looks away from society and culture, as there will be no expectation of finding Christ there. But that is a radically defective form of Christian doctrine. As we read in the New Testament:

> He is the image of the invisible God, the firstborn of all creation; for in him all things in heaven and on earth were created, things visible and invisible, whether thrones or dominions or rulers or powers – all things have been created through him and for him. He himself is before all things, and in him all things hold together. He is the head of the body, the church; he is the beginning, the firstborn from the dead, so that he might come to have first place in everything. For in him all the fullness of God was pleased to dwell, and through him God was pleased to reconcile to himself all things, whether on earth or in heaven, by making peace through the blood of his cross.
> (Col. 1.15–20)

Creation originates in and for the Word who became incarnate in Jesus Christ, and by his cross, all creation is reconciled and redeemed. To return to a theme from chapter 1, creation includes our relational and social being as human creatures: these are not layers of existence that we add on to our God-given condition as bare individuals, but intrinsic to our nature. Our households, our places of work, the communities in which we share, the societies in which we live – these too are included when the Scripture says that 'in him all things hold together', and 'through him God was pleased to reconcile to himself all things'. By following him in the whole of our lives as creatures participating within creation – trusting him, being united with him – we share in that redemption, even as sin continues to mark and mar our lives. Christ leads his followers amidst the complexities of creation's order which is now held together in him, the crucified and risen one, on the way to the coming of God's kingdom in its fullness, when he will be revealed and we with him (Col. 3.4). Discipleship is learning to understand the whole of our lives as human creatures within this reconciled yet still sin-warped creation that longs to obtain 'the freedom of the glory of the children of God' (Rom. 8.21), shaping them according to the pattern of human life revealed in Jesus Christ's incarnation, earthly ministry, death, resurrection and ascension.

The centrality of seeking the kingdom for the life of discipleship is not only important in that it validates a wide arena of activities of the creaturely life in which we participate. Seeking the kingdom also reminds us that the transformation we long for does not rest on our striving alone, but in the mystery of how our actions and the actions of others might be useful to and utilized by God in pointing towards the new creation. A proper kingdom theology rests on the tension that we are called to pray and act for God's kingdom to become present and real to us now, confident that the kingdom is truly present and real beyond anything we can imagine in the crucified and risen Christ, yet longing too for the fullness of the kingdom that can only come with Christ's return and a new creation in which sin and death will be no more.

The church as community of disciples

It is as a community of kingdom-seeking disciples, therefore, that the church is the sign, instrument and foretaste of the kingdom of God, to return to the formulation that was used in the previous chapter.[87] This community seeks the reign of God as it does the will of God 'on earth as in heaven', which means in the whole of their earthly lives, across every part of political, social and cultural life – in short, in all the created pathways that humans live and walk every day. For by God's providence, structures outside the church have been established in and through which we may hear and receive the call to discipleship. These structures incorporate and ideally preserve and promote the gifts of creation, working through them to sustain orderly living in the land to which the Church of England is particularly called. In them we may expect to find and to enact signs of the coming kingdom of God, as well as encountering various forms of resistance to it. We are called to be faithful followers of Jesus as we take our part in families, educational institutions, healthcare organizations, enterprises, charities, job centres, housing associations, trade unions, political parties, retirement communities and all kinds of other forms of human relationship within society. That requires being ready to identify those ways in which political, social and cultural life is marked by resistance to God's reign on earth, not least through injustice of all kinds, as well as those ways in which it is marked by the signs of God's reign.

To treat the challenges here as of only marginal importance would mean abandoning the vision of Christ's person, work and reign that the Church's teaching presents to us. Inadequate approaches to discipleship go hand in hand with defective understandings of Christology, because what we think discipleship means will depend on who it is we commit ourselves to following. Attention to Christology is critical for the healing of our theological imagination, if those who define themselves as disciples are to see themselves as God's creatures called for God's purposes in God's world.

For Bonhoeffer, the life of discipleship was bound up with a Christology of Christ's ongoing presence and activity; as he wrote in *Ethics*, 'Christian life is participation in the encounter of Christ with the world.'[88] Hence engagement in the world – in the social forms which have arisen within creation – becomes a place to share in this encounter. Clive Marsh has made the case that much teaching in the church about following Christ in the world sets up, incorrectly, a notion of 'carrying Christ' or 'representing Christ', whereas what should be affirmed is that 'Jesus Christ needs to be understood as an active, living presence, though as one who confronts us.'[89] For Bonhoeffer, while the church is rightly understood to have a divine mandate to make God known, this is not the only 'mandate' through which God is active or encountered. Our task of faithful following may therefore involve being able to name where Christ is being disclosed in 'social forms of human experience' – family, nation, economic life, institutions of all kinds, friendships etc. In such activity, disciples do not act apart from the church but bear in their person the one church sent by Christ in the power of the Holy Spirit to all nations and every part of the life of nations. As we seek God's kingdom in all the earth, pursuing the pathways to reconciliation, redemption and healing on which we are called, we should expect to encounter Christ whom we are following, 'the kingdom in person' (*autobasileia*), the one in whom all things hold together.

The Church of England, established to be a presence in every place and in all dimensions of national life, has a particular calling to be a community of disciples where all are able to grow in the wisdom they need to fulfil this calling in the varied contexts where Christ has placed them for his service. Such wisdom is a gift from above, i.e. from God (James 3.17), but that does not mean it therefore comes to us instantly or automatically: to receive it requires attentiveness and discipline, which is the way of growth in understanding for us as human creatures. The association between wisdom and the Spirit of God in Scripture underlines the point that seeing things as they are is not possible for human persons without sharing in the life of the Triune God.

The gift of the Holy Spirit to the church at Pentecost is inseparable from the church's union with the Son of God crucified and risen. Jesus promises his disciples that 'the Advocate, the Holy Spirit, whom the Father will send in my name, will teach you everything, and remind you of all that I have said to you' (John 14.26), and that 'When the Spirit of truth comes, he will guide you into all the truth.... He will glorify me, because he will take what is mine and declare it to you. All that the Father has is mine. For this reason I said that he will take what is mine and declare it to you' (John 16.13–15). If we would know the mind of Christ as we look to find the right path in the midst of the disorientation Christians are bound to experience in a post-Christendom culture, then we must keep in step with the Spirit. For Christian doctrine, spirituality means life in the Spirit, and we cannot expect to be taught and guided in the way of Jesus Christ independently from our participation in that life: spirituality and ethics belong together in discipleship, inseparable from being filled with the Spirit and being 'transformed by the renewing of your minds, so that you may discern what is the will of God – what is good and acceptable and perfect' (Rom. 12.2).[90] How the disciplines of the spiritual life can form us as disciples to discern 'what is good and acceptable and perfect' in our daily lives is the focus for the next section of this chapter.

Formation on the frontline

Challenges for contemporary discipleship

Discipleship has never been easy, yet social and cultural changes over the past hundred years have created some distinctive challenges. Attending to Christ to learn from him, become like him and live every moment with him requires setting aside time, as it always has, but now in a society when for many people time feels enormously pressurized by the ordinary demands of relational commitments, social roles and, for church members, supporting the church's activities. For many, the demands of paid work take up a much greater proportion of time than would have been the case for their parents and grandparents, while outside working hours we receive endless offers of new cultural products for our time-consuming consumption. The sabbath rhythm of work and rest, presented in the Scriptures as one way in which human practice is to image the divine creator, is difficult to sustain. Faced with these pressures, in the case of many who would be thought of as core church members, participation in activities that might be regarded as crucial for forming us as disciples and enriching our theological imagination, such as public worship, the sacraments, private prayer, scriptural reading, and Christian fellowship, might occupy on average little more than an hour a week.

At the same time, Christians are also needing constantly to navigate the crossing of different spheres of social existence, in many of which Christian faith may feel irrelevant or unwelcome, as discussed in the Introduction. The estrangement experienced between the practice of faith and everyday engagement with different communities and institutions means that the dynamic movement between being with Christ and walking with Christ that was presented in the previous section as characterizing discipleship is hard to sustain. Part of what is meant by the concept of 'post-Christendom', introduced in chapter 1, is that although in a country like England the influence of Christianity continues to be extensive in many kinds of ways, the vision of a profoundly Christian society in which growing up and living within the culture could be happily interwoven with following Christ and growing towards maturity in him has now ceased to have purchase. If the influence of Christianity is still apparent, so is the pull away from any sense of belonging to the church in terms of identity and from anything like credal orthodoxy in matters of belief: both are seen as minority options, not mainstream behaviour, and indeed statistically they clearly are, and ones that continue to diminish.

Some of the trajectories in our culture that draw us away from faithful discipleship may be relatively easy to identify, but there are also currents running within our society that are likely to elicit the perplexity identified in the Introduction, partly because we are unsure how we should evaluate them, and partly because we may not entirely appreciate how they are already affecting us. When institutions are losing security and trust but there is also pervasive pressure to show why we should be noticed, heeded, appointed or promoted rather than others, we can easily feel driven to engage in constant self-promotion and the search for competitive advantage. That can apply to worshipping communities and clergy as much as to secular organizations and their employees. Is it possible to resist this tendency, without simply accepting the ebbing away of our influence in the world around us as a necessary price to pay?

As was observed in the Introduction, our society, like every society, fosters through its practices particular ways of understanding human worth and fulfilment, for instance in relation to work. What work is most desirable, what work is most critical, and what work is most worthy of financial reward – and should the answer be the same in each case? The experience of the Covid-19 pandemic may have shifted some of our perceptions in this regard, as mentioned in Chapter 1, by highlighting our dependence day by day on those who do jobs associated with low levels of pay as well as respect and recognition, such as shop workers, bus drivers, postal workers and refuse collectors. How do we view those who appear at least to have less capacity to do work than others – the very young, the very old, those whose abilities and limitations mark them out from the majority? Those who seek to follow Christ day by day are still bound to be affected by what is presented within the culture they inhabit as desirable, worthwhile and bringing fulfilment, whether they consciously embrace it, consciously resist it or absorb it without noticing. They need to be able to find space to ask the question: are these ways of understanding human worth and fulfilment drawing me in a direction that converges with the path on which Christ is leading me – Christ who is also present in the muddled and sinful culture of which I am a part, Christ who will judge that culture and all who share in it and who calls me today in and to that culture, not to be somewhere else?

Disciplines of Christian formation

In his book on discipleship, Rowan Williams highlights Jesus' exchange with some of the disciples in the opening chapters of John's Gospel, where they ask him: 'where are you staying?' (John 1.38). Choosing to stay, or abide, is not about 'turning up from time to time…it's a commitment,' he writes; discipleship is 'about how we live; not just the decisions we make, not just the things we believe, but a state of being'.[91] The struggle we all face in our different contexts is how to sustain that state of being – or perhaps better, how to grow more fully into it in every part of our lives. How does attending to Jesus as our Lord and teacher become 'a state of being', a way of life, that encompasses everything?

As noted in the previous section, to find our way through the challenges of discipleship in the contemporary context, we need 'the wisdom from above' (James 3.17), as the gift of God that is especially associated with the Spirit of God, and we cannot evade the demands that receiving that wisdom will make upon us. In the words Jesus speaks to his disciples in John's Gospel at his final meal with them, following him through the saving mystery of his death and resurrection means a relationship of mutual indwelling, he in us and we in him. To understand this relationship, we have to know that the Father is in the Son and the Son is in the Father, and that the Son who is with us and indwells us sends the Spirit from the Father to be also with us and in us: 'And I will ask the Father, and he will give you another Advocate, to be with you for ever…. You know him, because he abides with you, and he will be in you' (John 14.16–17). It is through this indwelling by 'the Spirit of truth' that we receive the wisdom from above, an indwelling that remains inseparable from following Jesus, from discipleship as a 'state of being', listening to his words and enacting them: 'Those who love me will keep my word, and my Father will love them, and we will come to them and make our home with them' (John 14.23). What is asked of us is to keep his word, and this requires our memory, understanding and will.

Formation is a term that has been associated in Christian contexts especially with intensive periods of preparation for beginning ordained ministry or religious life. There are good reasons for expecting that such periods need to be marked by both a commitment to certain practices and disciplines and a receptiveness to the shaping work of the Holy Spirit. Yet insofar as this is about formation in the likeness of Christ, it cannot be different in kind from the formation that is required of every person who wishes to follow the way of Christ: for all of us, at all times, we need to be trained in readiness to respond to what is being asked of us, and that requires the same combination of commitment and receptiveness.[92]

Such formation for discipleship has traditionally been framed in terms of duties and disciplines that train us in attentiveness to Christ. We live in a culture within which there can be suspicion of such language as implying a kind of subordination to authoritative figures or institutions that is inimical to freedom and therefore human flourishing, but we also have a teacher who tells us: 'Take my yoke upon you, and learn from me; for I am gentle and humble in heart, and you will find rest for your souls. For my yoke is easy, and my burden is light' (Matt. 11.29–30).

Discipleship is inseparable from discipline, in the sense of practices that help learning from and about Christ to become part of the fabric of our lives – how we think, how we talk, how we relate to others and how we make decisions. The point of such disciplines is not to take us away from the frontline of discipleship in the world to find security in some sheltered 'spiritual' space outside it, but to foster in us the constant vigilance that Jesus speaks about in the Gospels: we need to be continually alert in every aspect of our lives to what may be pulling us away from the path of Christ, and to what is drawing us further along it and towards deeper encounter with him. While some may find the military metaphor implicit in 'frontline' unhelpful, its use here is intended to underline the theme in Jesus' teaching of his disciples that the kingdom's arrival precipitates struggle with the forces opposed to it[93] – forces that cannot be simplistically equated with a fixed group of people, or with certain social institutions or forms of culture, not least because the resistance will also come from within ourselves. If we believe, as was urged in the first chapter, that human society is part of the earth God made to be good, to pray for God's kingdom to come on earth is to offer ourselves as those through whom this prayer may be answered in the societies of which we are a part, not to ask for our withdrawal from them.

It is worth remembering that the monastic movement that shaped so much of Christianity's spiritual tradition was originally conceived as taking people into a place of intensified struggle against evil and striving for the kingdom. Strong disciplines of discipleship were perceived to be needed for monastic life because of the monks' consequent exposure to trial and temptation. This was bound up with the lay character of monasticism in its early forms: the institutional life of the church with its dioceses and bishops, though not without its besetting sins, protected people from the heat of the spiritual battle in certain respects. A strong case could be made that today it is those who spend the highest proportion of their lives in the 'secular' spheres of our society who have special need for the disciplines of discipleship, to help them seek the reign of God day by day in the place to which God has called them.

Anglican approaches

It became customary to understand the monastic state in terms of acceptance of a 'rule of life', such as the Rule of St Benedict, which by the end of the first millennium constituted the basic point of orientation for monastic communities across Western Europe. Clergy associated with cathedrals were called 'Canons' because they were obliged to live under a common rule of life of this kind (the Greek loan word 'canon' meaning 'rule'). Such clergy continued to be referred to in this way in the post-Reformation Church of England, even though no more was generally required of them than of others. It remains the case in the Church of England, however, that some of what one might expect historically to find in a monastic rule of life is indeed still required of the clergy as a matter of Canon Law, such as weekly attendance at the eucharist and daily participation in morning and evening prayer. One might also argue that the outline of such a rule is clearly present in the promises made by those being ordained.

It is hardly the case, however, that only those with a ministerial vocation to one of the three orders of ministry have need of the disciplines of discipleship. The post-Reformation Church of England expected the whole people of God to gather in the parish church to share in morning and evening prayer on a daily basis, as well as being present for Holy Communion on Sundays. The sevenfold daily office, recited in Latin, that was followed in the medieval period was hardly compatible with the working patterns and education of the great majority of the population. Hence, creating a pattern for public daily prayer in which all could participate, in which the Psalter was recited monthly and the whole Bible read through every year, was foundational for Cranmer's vision of a reformed

Church of England, as noted in the previous chapter, however flawed and unrealistic that aspiration may have been in various respects.

Another innovation, paralleled in other parts of Western Christianity in the sixteenth century, was requiring candidates for confirmation to learn the Catechism and formally make the answers to the questions it contained: for the first time, those who had been baptized as infants were required to make public promises for themselves about following the way of Christ. To some extent this is paralleled in the 'Commission' within contemporary services of baptism and confirmation for the Church of England, which includes the questions, 'Will you continue in the apostles' teaching and fellowship, in the breaking of bread, and in the prayers?', and 'Will you persevere in resisting evil, and, whenever you fall into sin, repent and return to the Lord?'[94] The Church of England has, then, been clear in its liturgy that baptism entails discipleship and discipleship requires certain disciplines.

It would, however, be misleading to imply that recognition of the importance of attending to the formation of the whole people of God suddenly emerged with the Protestant Reformation. Indeed, it would be possible to argue that the zeal of the English Reformers in the sixteenth and seventeenth centuries, from Thomas Cranmer to Jeremy Taylor, to draw every member of the church more deeply into following Christ continued and intensified reforming energies already becoming evident in Catholicism towards the end of the Middle Ages.[95] Nonetheless, the rich tradition of the Church of England in this regard indicates that concern for the formation of every Christian is deeply and properly Anglican, as is attention to the social and cultural dimensions of that formation.[96]

It is perhaps true that pastors and teachers in the Church of England have become less clear and less confident in setting out what pattern of disciplines might fit with discipleship in the contemporary context. Part of the picture here is a late-modern culture in which any guidance from people in positions of authority is liable to be viewed with suspicion if not simply ignored. It may be appropriate to find a new language, for instance advocating practices that have been passed down as part of the tradition of Christian discipleship as commitments that can liberate us to grow in the knowledge of Christ, rather than duties to which members of the church should be expected to conform. Some prefer to talk about a 'rhythm' rather than a 'rule' of life. Failure on the part of the clergy, however, to encourage habits of daily prayer and Bible reading among all the baptized in the Church of England, when many continue to assume that it is part of their duty to maintain such habits themselves, is itself an expression of clericalism, however much it might be felt as a kind of spiritual leniency. Are all not disciples together of the one Lord, bound by the same baptismal promises? This is not to deny that lay people may collude with a clericalizing mentality that regards ordained ministers as practising discipleship on behalf of the rest of us, or with a seriousness that cannot realistically be expected of the rest of us.

Of course, there is a danger of idealizing the past. The disciplines of discipleship referred to in relation to Cranmer's reforming work pivot on the parish church as the place of daily Christian assembly. There are practical reasons why, for many of us, that is unworkable, and one might ask whether the lingering ideal of English Christendom in this respect has made it easy for something of a spiritual vacuum to emerge in its place. Puritan spirituality gave a great deal of emphasis to the household as the site of formation for discipleship, with gatherings for daily worship, bible study and intercession, but the post-Restoration Church of England was keen to distance itself from this legacy. It is not simply, however, a matter of convenience. In our post-Christendom society marked by the dynamics of secularization, it is important that the disciplines of discipleship train us in attentiveness to Christ across the different social domains we inhabit. That should certainly involve bringing those domains into the Sunday assembly – sermons and intercessions, most obviously – as well as smaller church groups and individual times of prayer. The Ignatian tradition of the *examen* at the end of every day, examining where throughout the day I have drawn close to Christ and where I have been indifferent or unheeding, continues to be a valued practice for responding to Ignatius' exhortation to his first followers to 'seek God our Lord in all things... loving him in all creatures and all creatures in him'.[97]

Everyday discipleship

There is also, though, an obvious case for locating some discipleship practices within those various domains that we shuttle between day by day: saying grace with the people we share meals with, inside and outside the home; studying the scriptures on the morning commute; praying with colleagues in the workplace. There is an extensive body of resources that can be drawn on for this, from Christian tradition as well as contemporary practice; the Evangelical Revival, for instance, gave renewed attention in the eighteenth and nineteenth centuries to household prayer. Of course, different practices will be appropriate in different circumstances. But the reason for stressing it here is that the implication of the analysis in this report is that for the healing of our theological imagination, we need spiritual practices that can help us counter the restriction of spirituality to a zone that is closed off from the everyday world.[98] We need habits that can train us in attentiveness to the presence of the Christ we follow in every dimension of our lives, above all in those aspects where it may seem difficult to name it or even discern it. We need a spirituality of discipleship that draws on the riches of the church's Christology, so that it can draw us into the fullness of the mystery of Christ, rather than allowing it to be confined only to certain spaces in our lives and thereby ultimately denied.

Formation for discipleship, then, cannot simply be about what happens away from those contexts where the path of Christian discipleship may be hard to discern, but it must become a living reality within them. For each such context is an aspect of our God-given reality as human creatures where the kingdom can draw near, even as evil can also encroach upon us. The disciplines of discipleship that are needed must therefore include ways of learning to imagine and so see our participation in society and culture, however 'secular' it may seem and claim to be, as integral to our discipleship, and not as an interruption of it: as a place where Christ is present as one whom we can meet, serve and follow.

The learning that is integral to discipleship is therefore about understanding the ways that faith permeates all of life, bringing healing to oneself and to others. There is a role here for catechesis as the initial formation of disciples, where learning might be transformative by provoking new patterns of thinking and acting. However, Christian learning must also go further to seek to provide ways for helping people to enter into deeper patterns of theological reflection on their own experience of God, and of their experience of trying to follow his call.[99] As Jeff Astley and others have shown, this ought to begin from the ordinary experience and conversation about faith, with the familiar language people use to describe and talk about God, as well as deepening more formal theological knowledge.[100]

Discipleship and the diversity of vocations

Solidarity in discipleship

All God's people are called to the way of discipleship. That call is inseparable from baptism, as the Church of England's liturgies for baptism and confirmation make clear. For all of us, whatever our place within the body of Christ, it begins and ends here. A renewed sense of the profound solidarity of discipleship should be one of the outcomes of the pathways to healing for our theological imagination that have been identified in this report.

In chapter 1, it was proposed that social, relational and ministerial vocations should be regarded as different ways of living out the one call to follow Christ, ways which are neither mutually exclusive nor to be set in some kind of hierarchy. Indeed, all disciples, whatever vocations they may recognize and receive from God's hand, must learn the way of Jesus in their social roles and responsibilities, in their households and closest relationships, and in their service of others within the body of Christ. The church as a community of disciples should make space for all to grow in each of these areas, through encouragement and challenge. There is a fundamental solidarity therefore in how vocational questions are framed. Continual vigilance is needed against the temptation that is never far away to regard some vocations as the better ones. Some might be viewed as paradigmatic for truly serious discipleship, and others as best fitted for those happy to occupy the lower divisions of the Christian life. Some might be presumed to merit the church's attention and support, while others are be passed over as individual options that come without any great spiritual demands. Some vocations might be seen as marking those who receive them as really having Christ's call upon their life, while other Christians are free from the associated responsibilities and privileges. But the truth is that we are all called to the way of discipleship, and there is no higher calling.

Chapter 2 faced directly one of the catalysts for this report, the perception that the Church of England has a specific problem in framing the relationship between ordained ministries and other ministries, such that the former always end up being valued at the expense of the latter. Solidarity in discipleship as the great adventure to which all are called should help us to resist the tendency to put more weight on 'ministry' than it merits, as if this term somehow exhausts

Christ's work in the world: ministries – always in the plural, ordained and lay – are part of it, and a necessary part, as each with the gift they have been given builds up the body, but only a part. The impoverishment of ecclesiological imagination that shrinks the church to a social institution is likely to result in placing an excessive theological value on institutional leadership, associated for a variety of reasons with the clergy. Where the church is constantly pictured through spatial language, it will be easy to locate its theological centre in the place where the worshipping community regularly meets, and therefore to attribute a corresponding ecclesiological centrality to those whose everyday life revolves around it to a greater degree than is the case with others. To see the church as the community of missionary disciples, as advocated in this chapter, helps us to grasp that dynamic interplay of witness to Christ in all the world and communion with one another in Christ is constitutive of its being, its true centre.

Ministries given for the sake of discipleship

The point of such reimagining is not to make ministries in general, or ordained ministries in particular, less important, but to give them their proper importance, which is to ensure this dynamic interplay can unfold to the glory of God. Ministerial vocations are not the highest form of discipleship, but rather given by Christ to the church for the sake of discipleship. The verses from Ephesians 4 that were discussed in some detail in chapter 2 need to be read also in the light of what follows them. Thus, 'the gifts he gave were that some would be apostles, some prophets, some evangelists, some pastors and teachers,' and all are to the end of bringing the body of Christ 'to the unity of the faith and of the knowledge of the Son of God, to maturity, to the measure of the full stature of Christ' (Eph. 4.11–13). For members of the body, the end is faithful, attentive following of Christ that desires nothing other than to be with him where he is and to know him as he is. All ministries, therefore, need to be oriented together to discipleship. To quote again from 'Ministry for a Christian Presence':

> The Church's licensed, authorised and commissioned ministers, ordained and lay, national and local, are called and equipped to build up the Body of Christ to witness to God's love and work for the coming of his kingdom. They are all called to be disciple-making disciples.

> Ordained and lay ministers teach and equip lay people to follow
> Jesus confidently in every sphere of life in ways that show the
> difference the Gospel makes. They recognize that all are baptized
> into Christ, complementary in gifts and vocation, mutually
> accountable in discipleship, and equal partners in mission.[101]

Those who, in the Ephesians 4 passage, are to be equipped by God's gifts
are described as 'saints': people made holy by union with Christ, in whom the
sanctifying Spirit dwells. The 'unity of the faith and of the knowledge of the Son
of God' in verse 13 should not be separated from the 'unity of the Spirit' in verse
3. Ministry, as the work of 'building up the body of Christ', must recognize the
sanctifying work of the Holy Spirit in the members who make up that body as
the condition and the horizon for all such endeavour. Any movement towards
the kingdom of God comes from the agency of the Spirit and is never
something we can claim or control for ourselves.

One aspect of the distinctiveness of ministerial vocation then becomes the
responsibility it brings with it for supporting other disciples in discerning and
living out their vocations, including their relational and social vocations. For
most Christians, most of the time, discipleship is lived out in close relationships
and social engagement. Participation in worshipping communities and spiritual
practices needs to nourish them and equip them for those. One of the critical
questions for discipleship will be discerning when following Jesus means
embracing a commitment to this person or community, or to this form of
work or institutional context. As was stressed in the first chapter, worshipping
communities should be relational networks where reflecting on such questions
together, and supporting those who may be struggling with them, is a normal
part of what goes on. Those who are licensed or commissioned as ministers
for the church have a shared responsibility to ensure that is the case, enabling
the gifts of all to be used for the common good. The role of Christian ministers
in supporting the discipleship of all God's people must therefore involve a
responsibility to address the weaknesses that have been identified in this
report as hampering the participation of all God's people in all God's work,
relieving our theological anaemia with the fullness of Christ's wisdom.

Coming to judgment

One of the strong cultural currents in our society is the upholding of autonomy as a final value – autonomy in the sense that it is always best for me to come to my own decision on my own terms about what it is right for me to do, without reference to any external authority. Any opposition to such a stance can appear to slide into authoritarianism or some form of collective control. Once that way of seeing things is accepted, however, there is a real risk of simply giving up on the challenges of seeking to form moral and spiritual judgments as a church about what is happening in our society and culture. Where this happens, however, we also give up on the church as a community of disciples, called to be the sign, instrument and foretaste of God's reign and therefore to judge, with due care and humility, where there is resistance to that reign. We also give up on the church as the fellowship of the Holy Spirit, the giver of wisdom from above. Life in the Spirit, the source of both spirituality and ethics in Christian discipleship, is always life together. In responding to the inevitable perplexities of being disciples in a post-Christendom context, we therefore need to work at developing practices of listening together, thinking together, and discerning together 'what is the will of God – what is good and acceptable and perfect' (Rom. 12.2).

The healing pathway we need to follow here relates closely to the healing of the theological imagination that was emphasized with regard to the first critical factor mentioned in the Introduction. As we become more confident in understanding society and culture as an integral part of God's good creation, hallowed and vindicated by Christ himself though deeply marred by human sin, so we can also begin to see more clearly what are the good purposes that different aspects of society and culture are given to fulfil, and where these are being frustrated. As we practise daily discipleship in the various contexts of our everyday life, seeking to meet Christ there, so we can sense more keenly where his presence and reign are being rejected. This remains, however, an ecclesial endeavour, and not simply an individual one: we need to address the challenges together, seeking the wisdom of the Spirit together, and drawing on the gifts of those with different vocations, social, relational and ministerial. Again, those who have been called to responsibilities for teaching, preaching and making disciples have a critical role to play, but it cannot be undertaken without listening to the voices of those who hold responsibilities in quite different contexts. Here too, working as one body, filled with the Spirit of the risen Christ, full of hope and joy, we can encourage one another, praying 'Your kingdom come, your will be done, on earth as in heaven.'

Challenges for discipleship

This chapter has argued that fostering an understanding of discipleship as being with Christ and seeking his reign in every part of our lives is vital for healing our theological vision of what is true and good amidst the disorientation post-Christendom brings for the church.

To do that, we face significant challenges.

- As the one through whom and for whom all things exist and in whom all things now hold together, Christ's presence cannot be limited to religious institutions and activities. The Christology at the heart of the Church's doctrine is in direct tension with the privatization of religion that affects thinking and behaviour throughout our society – including that of Christians. We have to accept that to live in every walk of life consistently as public followers of Christ the Lord is hard and cuts against the grain.

- To follow Christ is to attend to him continually. To sustain our attention, we need the traditional disciplines of discipleship, as sometimes summarized in a rule of life. To regard these as matters of duty for the clergy and interest only for others is a legacy of clericalism. They are essential for living out our baptismal promises and our baptismal commission, and they need to be taught accordingly.

- The disciplines of discipleship need to train us for being with Christ and seeking his reign in every part of our lives, and not to be associated with retreat to some special zone of devotion. To do this, we need creative wisdom to re-shape the spiritual resources of Christian tradition for our own time. The challenge is to work out how to share in this vital spiritual work together.

- 'Spirituality' and 'ethics' have tended to become separated domains, in academic study as in institutional life. Yet life in the Spirit and discerning what is true and good belong together in the way of discipleship: we cannot have one without the other. We need to nurture networks where the ethical questions we encounter in our daily discipleship and the entire ethos of our culture are thought about so that they can be addressed prayerfully and actively together in the light of the Scriptures.

Conclusion: Kingdom Calling

This report has been framed as a plea for the healing of our theological imagination. The challenge identified in the Introduction was that good theology regarding the vocation, ministry and discipleship of the whole people of God has been presented many times over the past hundred years, with a particular weight of attention since the 1960s. Yet in the case of the Church of England at least, such theology has struggled to achieve a sustained and consistent purchase in the thinking, praying, planning and living of clergy and laity alike. We are bound to 'picture' who we are in relation to others, both human and divine, and if we do not make appropriately careful use of the images given to us for this purpose in the Scriptures to nurture a properly theological imagination, then we are likely to become captive without realizing it to pictures whose perspective comes from elsewhere. Failings in such theological imagination are one of the reasons that good theology in this area has not borne consistent fruit in practice and experience. In seeking to address this, the kingdom of God has emerged as a recurring theme throughout the text. It has not been assigned to a chapter or section title, nor to a specific place in the three main chapters. Instead, it has, if not obviously at all points, served as a connecting thread that helps weave them together into a whole.

In the first chapter, we looked to the doctrine of creation as the basis for a social theology – a theology of human life in society – that can feed our theological imagination regarding how we see our participation in the various communities and institutions that frame our daily life. We affirmed that these communities and institutions are part of God's creation of humanity. As such, they have an orientation to God's good purposes in creation, as well as being caught up in the dynamics of human sin. We cannot respond wholeheartedly to God's call without being willing to shape the communities and institutions in which we participate in accordance with those purposes, and to resist what draws them towards lovelessness and injustice. For many of us, that will mean being ready to ask the question of social vocation as a primary issue for faithful living: should I accept a commitment to a specific institutional context, community of people or concrete task, as central to how I serve others day by day and contribute with them to the common good, in the place and time that God has set me?

One of the key messages of chapter 1 was that we should avoid turning the variety of vocations into a hierarchy of value: social, relational and ministerial vocations are not to be weighed against one another, as if one brought us closer to God than another, nor should rankings be set up within them. Nonetheless, the affirmation of social vocation has a particular power in addressing the weakness of theological imagination about everyday life. It frames our daily activities and interactions within the work of the divine creator and therefore our sharing in that work as human creatures. Creation is to be the dwelling place of God, the expression of God's reign, with humanity bearing the image of the divine ruler into every part of earthly life: to identify and accept a social vocation, therefore, is to grasp that *this* institution, *this* community, *this* task is a space in which to strive for the kingdom of God, here and now.

The second chapter situated enduring tensions around 'ministry' in the Church of England in the context of ecclesiology, arguing that there is a persistent tendency to reduce the horizons for our understanding of the church to a social institution, or a community of people meeting in a particular place, or even that place itself as the point of stability from which people come and go. The problem here is not to say that it is wrong to think of any of these things as 'church': the church is all these things, in one way or another, but it cannot be defined by them. What makes the church is the dynamic rhythm of communicating the gospel with the world and deepening communion with one another in Christ, so that particular ministries find their purpose in sustaining that rhythm, as they build up the body of Christ to strengthen witness to Christ. It is a rhythm that draws in all the gifts of all God's people. Within it, the continuity represented by the historic episcopate and those who are episcopally ordained to ministries of word and sacrament is neither superior to nor separable from the ever-changing diversity of ministries exercised by those who are not ordained. All who accept a ministerial vocation, whether lay or ordained, receive responsibility for discerning and animating the gift given to each within the one body of Christ for the common good.

The flourishing of the diversity of gifts and ministries is intrinsic to the church whose being flows from the indwelling of the Spirit poured out at Pentecost. The subject of 'lay ministry' is not one to which we should turn under pressure either of declining resources to finance professional ordained ministries, or of a reduction in the numbers of those willing to serve as priests in parishes whether stipendiary or self-supporting. A church where the question of ministerial vocation is not regularly asked of every congregation, with the answers expected to be commensurate with the abundance of God's gifts, is failing in a fundamental duty, and, as it fails to nurture the gifts needed for communicating the gospel with the world and deepening communion with one another, it can expect to diminish and dwindle.

The image of God's kingdom can help our imaginations here. The report has commended the formulation that the church is sign, instrument and foretaste of the kingdom. The power of this way of seeing the church will depend on our vision of the kingdom, which is why the relation between kingdom and creation is so important. God's reign is not about individual souls detached from embodiment, including embodiment in social relations and cultural life: it embraces the whole of creation, all that God made and saw to be good in the beginning. The church's being and purpose can only be grasped against this horizon, and the church serves as sign and instrument of the kingdom through the daily lives of its members, in their living out of social and relational vocations. The church is located in every situation where the followers of Christ are acting in ways, though always limited and flawed, that point towards the kingdom and make space for it to touch and shape human lives. It is not more real when believers gather for word and sacrament on a Sunday than when they are engaged in all manner of occupations every day of the week. The life of the church encompasses the gathering of believers for fellowship and their service in the world, because both of these are necessary for it to be the sign, instrument and foretaste of the reign of God: one cannot stand without the other.

The third chapter, focusing on discipleship, sought to face the challenge that the culture that we inhabit as the Church of England can be profoundly disorienting for us in seeking to respond faithfully to God's call and live as disciples of Christ. In some cases we may be well aware of that disorientation but struggle to know how to respond; in others we may have come to accept it and need to be made uncomfortable with any uncritical acquiescence to it, to sense the tensions with how we are called to be and act. We know we cannot live anywhere else than in our culture, and we know too that there are powerful dynamics within it that can draw us away from the way of Christ, not least with regard to how we think and behave about work, worth and fulfilment.

The chapter proposes that a renewed appreciation of discipleship is critical for how we address this challenge. Discipleship means attending to Christ and to his message in all things, in every circumstance: there is no situation in which we find ourselves where the gospel of Christ is not relevant, and there is no situation in which we find ourselves where Christ is not present with us, to teach us and guide us. We have to begin from this confidence of faith.

Understood in this way, discipleship is inseparable from the kingdom of God. Jesus opens his public ministry with the proclamation that the kingdom of God is near, and in his words and actions he makes clear that it draws near in and through him, by who he is as manifested in what he does. He is the kingdom, the one place on earth where God's reign is complete, transforming all with whom he comes into contact as they welcome the good news of the kingdom with gratitude, generating conflict with those who seek to stifle it or simply ignore it. With the resurrection, the eyes of Jesus' followers are opened to see in him the one by whom and for whom all things were made, so that with the acceptance of him as Lord, God's kingdom is restored in every part of creation.

Every calling, then, is a kingdom calling: in responding to God's address, we are seeking God's reign, seeing ourselves against its horizon and longing for its fullness to come. The calling of God's people as a whole is a kingdom calling: called to be sign, instrument and foretaste of the kingdom, which extends over all creation. Therefore, those who accept a vocation to ministry, to building up the body of Christ, also have a kingdom calling, because their vocation is to build up the body to be this sign, instrument and foretaste. That will mean caring for communities and institutions, including their resources, such as their buildings – but as spaces where the body can be strengthened for this purpose, always looking out beyond the community, the institution and the building to what defines its being: the kingdom of God come amongst us in Jesus Christ, which is the future of all creation.

That every calling is a kingdom calling also means there is an eschatological dimension to it, a pointing forward to the fullness that is to come in the new heavens and the new earth. That applies to social and relational vocations as well. The seeking for God's kingdom to come in the various spheres of our social existence will never reach fulfilment this side of the resurrection of the dead, but there are real opportunities for the church to be present there in its members as sign, instrument and foretaste of the kingdom. The use in Scripture of nuptial imagery for that fullness in the life of the age to come, and in Christian tradition of the angelic life to describe life under religious vows, testify to the relevance of the eschatological dimension to relational vocations too: commitments to share one's life with other people can come to serve as foretaste of the kingdom as well as sign and instrument, pointing towards the glorious truth that awaits us and already has power to transfigure our everyday lives here and now.

Every calling in Christ, then, is a calling towards the kingdom. It is also a calling of the kingdom: God's reign is itself an invitation, an opening. In order to receive it, we need to lift up our eyes to see how far it extends, and the space it provides for the vocation, ministry and discipleship of the whole people of God.

Afterword

by Stephen Cottrell

Archbishop of York

One of the most frustrating experiences is when we can see we have a problem but we aren't clear what is causing it or how we might solve it. Such has been the case with our failure to embrace the role of the laity in the mission of the Church.

This is why I am grateful to the Faith and Order Commission for their *Kingdom Calling* report. They have helped us to see with fresh eyes what the theological issues inhibiting the full flourishing of all God's people have been and how we can tackle them.

Kingdom Calling confronts the ways in which we have limited our vision of our calling, the church and our discipleship. It has shown us how we have allowed secularism and fears arising from that to restrict the scope of our Christian ministry, to diminish our confidence to witness in public life and to put too much emphasis on ordained ministry at the expense of recognising and embracing the gifts of the laity.

And *Kingdom Calling* gives us not only the diagnosis of what has gone wrong but also the key to our healing. It does this by drawing us back to the reality that we are called by God in creation to share God's work in the world and are set free by Christ to do so. Therefore, every Christian has a share in God's ministry and we rejoice in this.

We are reminded that it is important we recognize the variety of ministries each of us is called to exercise – social, relational and ministerial – and to celebrate the richness of these without creating a hierarchy. Ministry is about our life and witness in every aspect of our daily life – not just the things we do in church.

This report also challenges us to recognize that church is not just a place. Instead, it is the people of God seeking the kingdom of God in every area of life, being bold in that witness and willing to confront injustice and all things which diminish others.

As we plan our strategy for the next five years, *Kingdom Calling* shows us that we need to be far more proactive in helping people to think about their vocations and their commitments in all areas of life and to discern how these accord or not with following Christ. Our churches must be better at making the connections between the faith we celebrate on Sunday and the life we live on Monday and indeed the rest of the week.

We also need to equip people for their discipleship in daily life through a far greater focus on Christian formation. This will include learning to follow patterns of life and discipline including prayer, Bible reading and daily reflection.

At the heart of all this is our relationship with Christ. In the Gospels, the twelve people we call the disciples are the same twelve people we called the apostles. There is never a point they graduate from one to the other. They are always those who gather around Jesus and learn from him – disciples; and they are always those who are sent by Jesus – apostles.

Our whole life discipleship needs to have the same pattern of being gathered around Jesus to learn from him and being sent by Jesus to serve him in the world.

We have been given a great resource in *Kingdom Calling* which, building on earlier reports on discipleship and lay ministry including *Setting God's People Free* and *Calling All God's People*, has shed a clear and challenging light on what the issues are and what we need to do. I encourage all of us now to take its lessons to heart, and emboldened by the deeper theological vision it has given us, to embrace and encourage the ministry of all Christians as we look forward to the future.

Notes

1. Archbishops' Council, *Setting God's People Free: A Report from the Archbishops' Council*, GS 2056, 2017, available at https://www.churchofengland.org/sites/default/files/2017-11/GS%20Misc%202056%20Setting%20God%27s%20People%20Free.pdf, p. 5 (accessed 01/06/2020).

2. Archbishops' Council, *Setting God's People Free*, p. 13.

3. Lay Ministries Working Group, *Serving Together: The Report of the Lay Ministries Working Group 2015/16*, available at https://www.churchofengland.org/sites/default/files/2019-02/serving_together_report.pdf (accessed 09/07/2020).

4. Faith and Order Commission, *Calling All God's People: A Theological Reflection on the Whole Church Serving God's Mission* (London: Church House Publishing, 2019).

5. Martin Seeley, 'Ministry for a Christian Presence in Every Community', GS Misc 1224, 2019, available at https://www.churchofengland.org/sites/default/files/2019-06/GS%20Misc%201224%20Ministry%20for%20a%20Christian%20Presence.pdf (accessed 01/06/2020).

6. Seeley, 'Ministry for a Christian Presence', p. 1.

7. Archbishops' Council, *Setting God's People Free*, pp. 8–9.

8. The project is expected to publish its findings in November 2020.

9. Yves Congar, *Lay People in the Church: A Study for a Theology of Laity*, trans. Donald Attwater (London: Geoffrey Chapman, 1965); Hendrik Kraemer, *A Theology of the Laity* (London: Lutterworth Press, 1958).

10. Vatican II, Gaudium et Spes, *Pastoral Constitution on the Church in the Modern World*, 1965, http://www.vatican.va/archive/hist_councils/ii_vatican_council/documents/vat-ii_const_19651207_gaudium-et-spes_en.html; Apostolicam Actuositatem, *Decree on the Apostolate of the Laity*, 1965, http://www.vatican.va/archive/hist_councils/ii_vatican_council/documents/vat-ii_decree_19651118_apostolicam-actuositatem_en.html.

11. Stephen Verney, *Fire in Coventry* (London: Hodder & Stoughton, 1964).

12. Kathleen Bliss, *We the People: A Book about Laity* (London: SCM Press, 1963).

13. Mark Gibbs and T. Ralph Morton, *God's Frozen People: A Book for – and about – Ordinary Christians* (London: Collins, 1964).

14. Commission on Evangelism, *Towards the Conversion of England: Being the Report of a Commission on Evangelism Appointed by the Archbishops of Canterbury and York pursuant to a Resolution of the Church Assembly Passed at the Summer Session 1943* (London: The Press and Publications Board of the Church Assembly, 1945).

15. Michael Ramsey (ed.), *Essays Written for the Lambeth Conference: Lambeth Essays on Ministry* (London, SPCK: 1968).

16. Jeremy Worthen, 'Priestly Formation through Part-time Study in the Church of England and its Relationship to Roman Catholic Developments', in Matt Ham (ed.), *Late Have I Loved You. Part-time Priestly Formation for Adults: Psycho-spiritual Aspects* (Lulu Press, 2011), pp. 40–51.

17. John Mantle, *Britain's First Worker-priests: Radical Ministry in a Post-war Setting* (London: SCM, 2000).

18. Anthony Russell, *The Clerical Profession* (London: SPCK, 1980); Derwyn Williams, 'Parsons, Priests or Professionals? Transforming the Nineteenth-Century Anglican Clergy', Theology 110 / 858 (2007), pp. 433–42.

19. Board of Education, *All Are Called: Towards a Theology of the Laity. Essays from a Working Party of the General Synod Board of Education* (London: CIO, 1985).

20. Ruth Etchells, *Set my People Free: A Lay Challenge to the Churches* (London: Fount, 1995), p. xiii.

21. Working Group of the Board of Education, *Called to New Life: The World of Lay Discipleship*, GS Misc 546 (London: Church House Publishing, 1999), p. 37.

22. Working Party on the Structure and Funding of Ordination Training, Archbishops' Council, *Formation for Ministry within a Learning Church*, GS 1496 (London: Church House Publishing, 2003).

23. House of Bishops and Archbishops' Council, *Challenges for the New Quinquennium: A Report from the House of Bishops and the Archbishops' Council*, GS 1815, 2011.

24. Archbishops' Council, *Setting God's People Free*, p. 1.

25. Charles Taylor, *A Secular Age* (Cambridge, Massachusetts: Belknap, 2007), pp. 423–37. The idea that we live in a secular age has been questioned by some; see for instance Martyn Percy, 'Many Rooms in my Father's House: The Changing Identity of the English Parish Church', in Steven Croft (ed.), *The Future of the Parish System: Shaping the Church of England for the 21st Century* (London: Church House Publishing, 2006), pp. 3–15.

26. José Casanova, *Public Religions in the Modern World* (Chicago: University of Chicago Press, 1994).

27. Faith and Order Commission, *Witness* (London: Church House Publishing, 2020).

28. Cf. Pope John Paul II, Laborem Exercens, 1981, http://www.vatican.va/content/john-paul-ii/en/encyclicals/documents/hf_jp-ii_enc_14091981_laborem-exercens.html, §§1–5.

29. Cf. House of Bishops, *Living in Love and Faith: Christian Teaching and Learning about Identity, Sexuality, Relationships and Marriage* (London: Church House Publishing, 2020), Part 3, Chapter 10, 'A Story about Being Human'.

30. James K. A. Smith, *Desiring the Kingdom: Worship, Worldview, and Cultural Formation* (Grand Rapids, Michigan: Baker Academic, 2009), p. 165.

31. Cf. Nicholas Lash, *The Beginning and End of 'Religion'* (Cambridge: Cambridge University Press, 1996).

32. Charles Taylor, *Sources of the Self: The Making of the Modern Identity* (Cambridge, Massachusetts: Harvard University Press, 1989).

33. The Doctrine Commission of the General Synod of the Church of England, *Being Human: A Christian Response to Personhood Illustrated with Reference to Power, Money, Sex and Time*, GS 1494 (London: Church House Publishing, 2003), p. 131.

34. Alistair I. McFadyen, *The Call to Personhood: A Christian Theory of the Individual in Social Relationships* (Cambridge: Cambridge University Press, 1990).

35. The quotation is from St Augustine of Hippo, as cited in Henri de Lubac, *The Splendour of the Church*, trans. Michael Mason (New York: Sheed and Ward, 1956), p. 133.

36. Lambeth Conference 1920, Resolution 9, 'Appeal to All Christian People', §I, https://www.anglicancommunion.org/resources/document-library.aspx?author=Lambeth+Conference&year=1920. Cf. Raymond Chapman, *Law and Revelation: Richard Hooker and His Writings, Canterbury Studies in Spiritual Theology* (Norwich: Canterbury Press, 2009), p. 67, citing Of the Laws of Ecclesiastical Polity: 'But a Church, as now we are to understand it, is a society; that is, a number of men belonging unto some Christian fellowship, the place and limits whereof are certain.'

37. Vatican II, Lumen Gentium, *Dogmatic Constitution on the Church*, 1964, §I, https://www.vatican.va/archive/hist_councils/ii_vatican_council/documents/vat-ii_const_19641121_lumen-gentium_en.html.

38. Gustav Wingren, *Luther on Vocation*, trans. Carl C. Rasmussen (Eugene, Oregon: Wipf and Stock, 2004), pp. 4–5.

39. The terminology used here needs to be understand as a kind of shorthand, whose sense relies on how it is explained in the report, as summarised in the preceding paragraph. Using the terms 'social' and 'relational' in a more general way, it could truthfully be said that all vocations are social and all are relational, given that they involve serving the common good alongside others. Some would also argue that all can be described as ministerial, a point that will be addressed in Chapter 2.

40. It is significant in this respect that the chapter on 'The Universal Call to Holiness' directly precedes the chapter on 'Religious' in Vatican II, Lumen Gentium; the former states emphatically that 'The classes and duties of life are many, but holiness is one – that sanctity which is cultivated by all who are moved by the Spirit of God, and who obey the voice of the Father and worship God the Father in spirit and in truth. These people follow the poor Christ, the humble and cross-bearing Christ in order to be worthy of being sharers in His glory' (§41).

41. L. M. Rulla, *Anthropology of the Christian Vocation*, Vol. 1, Interdisciplinary Bases (Rome: Gregorian University Press, 1986), e.g. pp. 284 and 310.

42. Gill Goulding, '"The Irreducible Particularity of Christ" – Hans Urs von Balthasar's Theology of Vocation', in Christopher Jamison (ed.), *The Disciples' Call: Theologies of Vocation from Scripture to the Present Day* (London: Bloomsbury, 2013), p. 128.

43. Lambeth Conference 1958, Resolution 113, https://www.anglicancommunion.org/resources/document-library/lambeth-conference/1958/resolution-113-the-family-in-contemporary-society-marriage.aspx (accessed 08/07/2020).

44. House of Bishops, *Living in Love and Faith*, Part 3, Chapter 12, 'A Story about Human Ways of Loving'.

45. Martin Luther, *To the Christian Nobility of the German Nation Concerning the Improvement of the Christian Estate*, 1520, The Annotated Luther Study Edition (Minneapolis: Fortress, 2016), p. 381.

46. David Hoyle, 'How Did the Reformation Develop the Theology of Vocation?', in Jamison (ed.), *Disciples' Call*, pp. 95–110.

47. E.g. *The Rule of St Benedict*, ed. Justin McCann (London: Burns Oates, 1952), Chapter 48, 'Of the Daily Manual Labour', pp. 110–113; Hugh of St Victor, *Didascalicon*, trans. Jerome Taylor (New York: Columbia University Press, 1961), pp. 152–54.

48. The response to the question, 'What is thy duty towards thy neighbour?' ends with 'to do my duty in that state of life, unto which it shall please God to call me.'

49. *Common Worship: Daily Prayer* (London: Church House Publishing, 2005), p. 542.

50. *Board of Education, All Are Called*, p. 3.

51. Pope John Paul II, *Laborem Exercens*, §9.

52. See Nicholas Townsend, 'Transcending the Long Twentieth Century: Why We Should and How We Can Move to a Post-Capitalist Market Economy', in Jeremy Kidwell and Sean Doherty (eds), *Theology and Economics: A Christian Vision of the Common Good* (New York: Palgrave Macmillan, 2015), pp. 199-218, especially pp. 208-09.

53. Malcolm Brown (ed.), *Anglican Social Theology* (London: Church House Publishing, 2014).

54. Thomas Aquinas, *Summa Theologiae II-II*, q 189, a. 10.

55. Cf. David Lonsdale, *Eyes to See, Ears to Hear: An Introduction to Ignatian Spirituality* (London: Darton, Longman and Todd, 2000), pp. 89–109; Suzanne G. Farnham, Joseph P. Gill, R Taylor McLean and Susan M. Ward, *Listening Hearts: Discerning Call in Community* (New York: Morehouse, 2011).

56. Cf. Michael Banner, *The Ethics of Everyday Life: Moral Theology*, Social Anthropology, and the Imagination of the Human (Oxford: Oxford University Press, 2014).

57. Simon Foster, What Helps Disciples Grow?, Saltley Faith and Learning Series 2, 2016, available at https://www.saltleytrust.org.uk/publications/.

58. Taylor, *Sources of the Self*, pp. 368–90.

59. Frances Young, *Arthur's Call: A Journey of Faith in the Face of Severe Learning Disability* (London: SPCK, 2014).

60. John N. Collins, *Diakonia, Re-interpreting the Ancient Sources* (Oxford: Oxford University Press, 2009).

61. See Loveday Alexander, 'Diakonia, the Ephesian Comma, and the Ministry of All Believers,' in Jason Whitlark, Bruce Longenecker *et al.* (eds), *Interpretation and the Claims of the Text: Resourcing New Testament Theology* (Waco: Baylor, 2014), pp. 159-175.

62. On this question, see the discussion in Faith and Order Advisory Group, *Mission and Ministry of the Whole Church: Biblical, Theological and Contemporary Perspectives*, GS Misc 854 (London: Church House Publishing, 2007), pp. 113–24.

63. Faith and Order Commission, *Calling All God's People*, e.g. pp. 15–18.

64. Faith and Order Commission, *Calling All God's People*, p. 7.

65. Archbishops' Council, *Setting God's People Free*, pp. 8–12.

66. Cf. Karl Löwith, *Meaning in History: The Theological Implications of the Philosophy of History* (Chicago: University of Chicago Press, 1949); Franz Rosenzweig, *The Star of Redemption*, trans. Barbara Galli (Madison, Wisconsin: University of Wisconsin Press, 2005), pp. 301–306.

67. International Missionary Council, 'Statement on the Missionary Calling of the Church', Willingen, 1952; printed in Michael Kinnamon and Brian E. Cope (eds), *The Ecumenical Movement: An Anthology of Key Texts and Voices* (Geneva: World Council of Churches, 1997), p. 340.

68. Lesslie Newbigin, *The Open Secret: An Introduction to the Theology of Mission*, rev. ed. (Grand Rapids, Michigan: Eerdmans, 1995), p. 110. The roots of this formulation go back much earlier in Newbigin's writing and are already evident in the closing chapter of *The Household of God: Lectures on the Nature of the Church* (London: SCM, 1953), e.g. p. 145. For ecumenical texts, see for instance Anglican-Reformed International Commission, *God's Reign and Our Unity: The Report of the Anglican-Reformed International Commission 1981–1984* (London: SPCK, 1984), §29, p. 19, while the first section of *On the Way to Visible Unity: A Common Statement*, 1988, the basis for the Meissen Agreement between the Church of England and the Evangelische Kirche in Deutschland, is headed 'The Church as Sign, Instrument and Foretaste of the Kingdom of God' (available at https://www.churchofengland.org/sites/default/files/2017-11/The%20Meissen%20Agreement.pdf).

69. There is a rich vein of reflection on this theme in Roman Catholicism since Vatican II, where Lumen Gentium §11 affirmed that 'The family is, so to speak, the domestic church.'

70. Martin Connell, *Eternity Today: On the Liturgical Year*, Vol. 2, Sunday, The Three Days, The Easter Season, Ordinary Time (New York: Continuum, 2006), pp. 101–57.

71. *Common Worship: Ordination Services, Study Edition* (London: Church House Publishing, 2007), pp. 10, 32 and 55.

72. The General Synod of the Church of England, *On the Way: Towards an Integrated Approach to Christian Initiation* (London: Church House Publishing, 1995), Appendix 2, 'Extract from The Findings of the International Anglican Liturgical Consultation, Toronto, 1991,' pp. 124–25.

73. Anglican–Roman Catholic International Commission, *Walking Together on the Way: Learning to Be the Church – Local, Regional, Universal. An Agreed Statement of the Third Anglican–Roman Catholic International Commission* (ARCIC III) (London: SPCK, 2018), §52, pp. 24–25.

74. Seeley, 'Ministry for a Christian Presence', section 2, p. 3.

75. Stephen Pickard, *Theological Foundations for Collaborative Ministry* (Farnham: Ashgate, 2009), pp. 51–106.

76. *Common Worship: Ordination Services*, p. 79.

77. Seeley, 'Ministry for a Christian Presence', section 2, p. 2.

78. Norman Sykes, *Old Priest and New Presbyter: The Anglican Attitude to Episcopacy, Presbyterianism and Papacy since the Reformation* (Cambridge: Cambridge University Press, 1956), pp. 58–84.

79. Working Party of the House of Bishops, *For Such a Time as This: A Renewed Diaconate in the Church of England,* GS 1407 (London: Church House Publishing, 2001); Michael D. Jackson (ed.), *The Diaconate in Ecumenical Perspective: Ecclesiology, Liturgy and Practice* (Durham: Sacristy Press, 2019).

80. Seeley, 'Ministry for a Christian Presence', section 2, p. 2.

81. Sykes, *Old Priest and New Presbyter*.

82. Loveday Alexander and Mike Higton, *Faithful Improvisation? Theological Reflections on Church Leadership*, including the Report from the Church of England's Faith and Order Commission on Senior Church Leadership (London: Church House Publishing, 2006).

83. Dietrich Bonhoeffer, *Discipleship*, Dietrich Bonhoeffer Works vol. 4, ed. Geffrey B. Kelly and John D. Godsey, trans. Barbara Green and Reinhard Krauss (Minneapolis: Fortress Press, 2003), pp. 205–12.

84. See Linda Woodhead, 'The Challenges the C of E Reports Duck', *Church Times*, 23 January 2015, https://www.churchtimes.co.uk/articles/2015/23-january/comment/opinion/the-challenges-that-the-new-c-of-e-reports-duck. Cf. Angela Tilby, 'Dissing the D-word', Church Times, 30 January 2015, https://www.churchtimes.co.uk/articles/2015/30-january/comment/columnists/dissing-the-d-word, which claims that 'using the language of discipleship to describe the normal Christian life does not stand up particularly well to scriptural scrutiny.'

85. Loveday Alexander, 'The Church in the Synoptic Gospels and the Acts of the Apostles', in Paul Avis (ed.), *The Oxford Handbook of Ecclesiology* (Oxford: Oxford University Press, 2018), pp. 55–98; 'Discipleship and the Kingdom in the Gospels and Acts', in Stephen Cherry and Andrew Hayes (eds), *Discipleship: Then and Now* (London: SCM Press, 2020), forthcoming.

86. Steven Croft, 'Developing Discipleship', 2015, GS 1977.

87. On the church as community of disciples, see Avery Dulles, *Models of the Church*, expanded edition (New York: Doubleday, 1987), pp. 204–26. The term appears in Pope John Paul II, Redemptor Hominis, Encyclical Letter, 1979, http://www.vatican.va/content/john-paul-ii/en/encyclicals/documents/hf_jp-ii_enc_04031979_redemptor-hominis.html at §21; Pope Francis repeatedly refers to the church as 'a community of missionary disciples' in *Evangelii Gaudium: Apostolic Exhortation to the Bishops, Clergy, Consecrated Persons and the Lay Faithful on the Proclamation of the Gospel in Today's World*, 2013, http://www.vatican.va/content/francesco/en/apost_exhortations/documents/papa-francesco_esortazione-ap_20131124_evangelii-gaudium.html, e.g. §24. The slightly different phrase 'community of discipleship' appears in the convergence text on ecclesiology from the World Council of Churches' Commission on Faith and Order, *The Church: Towards a Common Vision*, 2013, § 2, http://www.oikoumene.org/en/resources/documents/wcc-commissions/faith-and- order-commission/i-unity-the-church-and-its-mission/the-church-towards-a-common-vision.

88. Dietrich Bonhoeffer, *Ethics*, ed. Eberhard Bethge, trans. Neville Horton Smith (London: Collins, 1964), p. 133.

89. Clive Marsh, *Christ in Practice: A Christology of Everyday Life* (London: Darton, Longman & Todd, 2006), p. 5.

90. Anglican – Roman Catholic International Commission (ARCIC) II, *Life in Christ: Morals, Communion and the Church*, 1993, §§4–32, available on-line at http://www.anglicancommunion.org/media/105236/ARCIC_II_Life_in_Christ_Morals_Communion_and_the_Church.pdf.

91. Rowan Williams, *Being Disciples: Essentials of the Christian life* (London: SPCK, 2016), p. 1.

92. Jeremy Worthen, *Responding to God's Call: Christian Formation Today* (Norwich: Canterbury Press, 2012).

93. E.g. Matt. 10.34–39, 12.22–29; Mark 6.7–13, 13.5–13; Luke 6.20–26.

94. *Common Worship: Christian Initiation* (London: Church House Publishing, 2006), e.g. p. 119.

95. Christopher M. Bellitto and Flanagin (eds), *Reassessing Reform: A Historical Investigation into Church Renewal* (Washington D.C.: Catholic University of America Press, 2012).

96. Peter H. Sedgwick, *The Origins of Anglican Moral Theology* (Leiden: Brill, 2019).

97. The Constitutions of the Society of Jesus and their Complementary Norms: A Complete English Translation of the Official Latin Texts (St Louis, Missouri: Institute of Jesuit Sources, 1996), p. 125. Compare the Common Worship Collect for the Sixth Sunday after Trinity: 'loving you in all things and above all things'.

98. Some resources to assist with this are provided on the 'Everyday Faith' pages of the Church of England website, at https://www.churchofengland.org/about/renewal-reform/setting-gods-people-free/everyday-faith (accessed 09/07/2020).

99. David Heywood, *Kingdom Learning: Experiential and Reflective Approaches to Christian Formation* (London: SCM Press, 2017).

100. Jeff Astley, *Ordinary Theology: Looking, Listening and Learning in Theology* (London: Routledge, 2002).

101. Seeley, 'Ministry for a Christian Presence', section 2, p. 3.